John W. Root

**Spain and it's Colonies**

John W. Root

**Spain and it's Colonies**

ISBN/EAN: 9783742810663

Manufactured in Europe, USA, Canada, Australia, Japa

Cover: Foto ©ninafisch / pixelio.de

Manufactured and distributed by brebook publishing software (www.brebook.com)

John W. Root

**Spain and it's Colonies**

# SPAIN

### AND

# ITS COLONIES

BY

## J. W. ROOT
**AUTHOR OF "TARIFF AND TRADE"**

LONDON
SIMPKIN, MARSHALL, HAMILTON, KENT, & Co. Ltd.
STATIONERS' HALL COURT, E.C.
1898

# PREFACE

———◆———

A DETAILED History of Spain and the Spanish Colonies is at present only to be gathered from a great number of scattered and disconnected volumes, and no attempt to write it in regular sequence could result in anything but a very bulky work. I have endeavoured, however, in the following pages, to give a brief yet comprehensive outline of the incidents which led, first to the rise, and then to the ignominious collapse of what ought to have been the greatest Colonial Empire the world has ever seen, and I have been specially careful to give prominence to such actions and policy as seem to me to have been pregnant with the greatest results.

Apart from any special interest which this little book may possess at the present moment, its contents may be found useful in illustrating more modern methods of colonial government. There are not a few people to-day who would reimpose some of the ancient restrictions where these are no longer binding, and still more who are unwilling to remove them where still in force; and it is just possible that an unprejudiced study of Spanish colonial history may induce such to reconsider their position.

J. W. R.

*May* 1898.

# CONTENTS

| CHAP. | | PAGE |
|---|---|---|
| I. | CONCEPTION | 9 |
| II. | EXPEDITION | 16 |
| III. | ACQUISITION | 23 |
| IV. | EXPLOITATION | 45 |
| V. | CONSOLIDATION | 53 |
| VI. | RESTRICTION | 61 |
| VII. | OPPOSITION | 69 |
| VIII. | EXPULSION | 85 |
| IX. | RETENTION | 95 |
| X. | SUCCESSION | 102 |

# SPAIN AND ITS COLONIES

───◆───

I

## CONCEPTION

IT is difficult to believe that the Power now wrestling with such ill success with its remaining colonial possessions, was once the discoverer and mistress of the Western Hemisphere. Well may we exclaim, " How are the mighty fallen!" as we view Spain almost on the point of being driven out of the New World, when, from San Francisco to the Straits of Magellan (or as they were for a time called the Straits of " Madre de Dios "), the nomenclature, and very frequently the language still in common use, betoken the former all-pervading influence of the Iberian monarchy. Perhaps it was never fitted for the work it undertook; it certainly never adapted itself to the requisite conditions in that distant empire, which fell to it more by accident than design, and which it always regarded more as a magazine of immediate utility than a trust for development and future advantage.

The four hundredth anniversary of the discovery of America was celebrated, it will be remembered, some six years ago by the World's Fair at Chicago. But what a different place Spain occupied in it, compared with the original event! The loan of a few trophies, instead of the ownership of a vast continent. Had Columbus foreseen the course events were destined to take, and the disasters that were to befall his adopted country, his troubled career would have been hastened to a still more premature end by chagrin, of which, indeed, he experienced quite enough as it was. But then, that great discoverer died unconscious of the fact that he had achieved anything of sufficient magnitude to alter the destinies of nations, much less create new ones, though no man then living set more value upon what he actually accomplished. He believed, however, that he had merely demonstrated the truth of the theories of many learned men, so enthusiastically adopted by himself, and opened up a new way to the most distant parts of the Old World, long traded with, both directly and indirectly, by the merchants of Venice and Genoa.

For many years he pored over maps and charts, and gathered every scrap of information relative to the existence of land in the West. Patriotism induced him at one time to place the fruit of his studies at the disposal of his native city; but Genoa being no longer in a position to undertake great enterprises, he first of all repaired to Portugal, as by far the most likely country to further his schemes. Ever since the time of Prince Henry the Navigator, in the early part of the fifteenth century, that little kingdom had been foremost in the work of exploration and discovery. The island of Madeira was touched in 1420, the Azores sighted and annexed in 1431. But it was along the African coast that Portuguese effort was mainly directed. Tradition asserted that the entire continent had been circumnavigated centuries before by voyagers from Phœnicia; but, as no details were recorded, the adventure was regarded as something more than dubious. However, the west coast began now to be systematically explored. Nuño Tristao entered the Senegal River in 1445; a year later Diniz Dias, a fellow-navigator, sailed as far as Cape Verde. The equator was not crossed until 1471, the Congo was revealed in 1484; and in 1486 the crowning feat of all was accomplished, when Bartholomew Diaz rounded the Stormy Cape, soon to become known as the Cape of Good Hope, and opened up communication with the East by water, instead of overland or by the indirect route of the Red Sea, which necessitated the transhipment of all merchandise conveyed that way.

Columbus arrived in Lisbon as early as 1470, and by his marriage with a lady, whose father and brother were both experienced navigators, his own ambitions were considerably stimulated. His expedition to the West was resolved upon in 1474, but was regarded by nearly everybody except himself as entirely visionary. He unfolded his plans to the then King of Portugal, John the Second, who, not liking to reject them on his own responsibility, referred them to a committee of experts, by whom they were reported on as extravagant. The fact is, they expected to accomplish by way of the East what Columbus proposed by sailing to the West; and the result proved them right, and entirely justified the opinion they formed of the latter's theories, though, as it turned out, it would have been greatly to the advantage of their country had they fallen into the error with him.

For ten years Columbus urged his views with more or less persistence, but with continually less prospect of success, as not only were the African expeditions absorbing attention, but John had himself secretly equipped an enterprise to sail westward, which resulted in failure, as most undertakings do when entered upon in a spirit of doubt, if not of positive disbelief. Disgusted at what appeared to Columbus an act of duplicity, as well as convinced that after what had happened there was little chance of prevailing, he quitted Lisbon, 1484, despatched his brother Bartholomew to enter into negotiations with Henry the Seventh of England, and after assuring himself that neither Genoa nor Venice were likely to lend him a willing ear, much less ready help, he repaired to the south of Spain in 1485.

Had Bartholomew not fallen into the hands of pirates, and so been prevented from reaching his destination for several years, it is more than probable that the credit as well as the profit of the discovery of America would have fallen at once to England, as Henry had both the means and the inclination to indulge in some such venture, provided it was not too costly, and showed any reasonable prospect of success. As it was, Christopher was left to pursue his weary pleadings before the Spanish Court, not, however, as in Portugal, without sincere and ardent well-wishers, who did their utmost to further his cause.

The circumstances of the two countries were entirely different. The smaller kingdom was already well on the way to secure the rich trade of the East, the larger one could only hope to thwart it by arriving first by another route. No more powerful sponsors could have been found than the Dukes of Medina Sidonia, and Medina Celi, who undertook to lay the case before Queen Isabella, to whom the latter nobleman sent Columbus armed with a letter of introduction, couched in the most seductive terms. It was an unfortunate time to put forward any proposals calculated to divert the wealth and strength of the kingdom beyond its own borders, for Ferdinand and Isabella were then in the very midst of the campaign which ended in the final overthrow of the Moorish dominion in the peninsula. Ferdinand, indeed, would have given them short shrift in any case; but there was a mutual sympathy between the Queen and Columbus which inclined her to lend a more ready attention, and eventually to concede all demands. Both, in short, were deeply religious, and though Columbus may have kept that part of his character somewhat in the background while in treaty with King John of Portugal, the revelation of it to his new patron was not inspired by self-interest, nor actuated by hypocrisy; and in the end the visionary schemes of converting the natives of the distant East to Christianity, and recovering the Holy Sepulchre from the grasp of the infidel, by means of the profits to be derived from the great trade that was to be opened up, had more to do with the discovery of the New World than any dreams of aggrandisement or lust of wealth.

Columbus had to travel many a thorny path before the goal of his ambition and desire was reached. Isabella never acted entirely on her own responsibility, even in the affairs of her own kingdom of Castile, without, at least, first consulting her consort; and Ferdinand, following the example of John, referred the whole matter to a council. The decision arrived at was the same, only the grounds upon which it was based were entirely different. Talavera, Bishop of Avila, and most of those who sat with him at the council board, professed to believe that the propositions of Columbus were a direct negation of biblical teaching regarding the shape of the earth; and the future discoverer found himself on the verge of a prosecution for heresy, not a risk to be lightly regarded in those days. The worst that happened to him was delay, but as the pressure of the Moorish War became greater, his prospects seemed to grow dimmer. Still, he had received more encouragement at the Court of Castile than anywhere else; and mainly through the influence of his friends, he was kept attached to it during its wanderings, and frequently formed part of the royal retinue, though he was given clearly to understand that his affairs could not receive further consideration until after the termination of the war. His patience at last exhausted, he was on the point of quitting the country almost unnoticed, when Juan Perez, at whose convent of La Rabida he sought shelter on his way to the coast, persuaded him to make one more attempt; and having been a former confessor of the queen, and on terms of intimate friendship with her, undertook to use his own good offices.

These were so far successful that Columbus was invited to return to the Court, then located in Granada, and, being fortunate enough to arrive just at the moment the stronghold of that kingdom capitulated, was all the more likely to be favourably dealt with during the general rejoicings that followed. No more difficulties indeed would have been placed in his way, had not his own extravagant demands inspired Talavera and his other opponents with fresh courage. Nothing less than appointment as perpetual and hereditary admiral and viceroy of any territories he discovered, together with a tenth of all the profits derived from them, would satisfy him; and so stubborn was he on that point, that negotiations were, as was supposed, finally broken off, and he left Santa Fé, the Spanish suburb of Granada, in February 1492, intending to proceed direct to France, and there solicit the good offices of the monarch of that kingdom.

That was exactly the way to rouse Spanish jealousy, and before he had proceeded any distance on his journey, he was again recalled, this time to be granted all his demands. The treasury was exhausted, it is true, and funds were scarce, but, in the enthusiasm of the moment, Luis de St. Angel, the receiver of ecclesiastical revenues, offered to advance whatever was needed, and Isabella, not to be outdone, expressed her intention of pawning the Crown jewels. The more phlegmatic Ferdinand regarded the whole business with contempt, and would have neither part nor parcel in it, with the result that the enterprise, according to stipulation, was undertaken solely for the benefit of Castile, and Ferdinand's neighbouring kingdom of Aragon was to share neither the expense nor the profit. That was a matter of small concern to Columbus, who, after eighteen years of weary waiting, now found his hopes about to be realised.

The agreement was duly drawn up by a royal officer, and a royal edict was placed in the hands of the overjoyed navigator, who hastened to the port of Palos to put it into effect. He had not foreseen the difficulties to be encountered there, but, after those already overcome, nothing could ever again daunt him, as he entertained no more doubt of what awaited him beyond the western sea than he did of his own existence.

## II

## EXPEDITION

WHEN so many learned men had condemned the schemes and ideas of Christopher Columbus, it was scarcely to be expected that the mind of the vulgar crowd would be captivated by them. It was one thing to be the holder of a royal edict of authorisation, and quite another to induce shipowners to risk their property in so foolhardy an enterprise, or mariners their lives on so mad an errand. Fortunately for Columbus, the little seaport of Palos lay, just at that time, under royal displeasure, and the penalty inflicted was to provide a ship for the voyage. There happened, too, to be in the port two enterprising brothers of the name of Pinzon, who were not only skilful navigators, but owned a vessel which they were willing should be included in the little squadron, while they themselves were also ready to embark in it; but their example did not prove contagious. The greatest difficulty was experienced in procuring a third vessel, as well as the crews to man and navigate them; and had not the most imperious orders been issued by the Court, the expedition would never have been equipped at all. In the long-run a very scratch armada was got together, consisting of two caravels and one larger vessel, the best of them little more than a leaky tub; and one hundred and twenty men were either cajoled or coerced into the service, few of whom ever expected to see their native shores again, while their relatives, in bidding them farewell, freely expressed the opinion that it was the last they would ever take.

It was a sorry spectacle, on the 3rd of August 1492, when the *Santa Maria*, the *Pinta*, and the *Niña*, weighed anchor and sailed to discover a new world. Gloom, instead of joy, overspread nearly every countenance. Twelve months' provisions were on board, but long before they were consumed, most of the seamen expected to have found a watery grave, if, indeed, they did not meet the worse fate of toppling over the abyss at the world's end. Columbus himself, as admiral of the fleet — save the mark! — commanded the *Santa Maria*; the two Pinzons, Martin Alonso, and Vicente Yañez, the *Pinta* and *Niña* respectively. The expressed object of the voyage was to convert the Grand Khan, supposed to be the great potentate of the far East, to Christianity; and Columbus never doubted but that in due course he would arrive at Japan, or Zipangu, as it had been named by the Venetian explorer, Marco Polo, who had reached it by an overland route more than a century before, and had described its wonders, together with those of Cathay or China, through which he passed on his way. The one condition imposed was, that the squadron should not touch at any place on the African continent, claimed to be under Portuguese jurisdiction, as that would have led to immediate hostilities between the two countries. King John could not credit that all the expense and trouble that had been gone to, were for so insane an object as had been given forth, and felt convinced that the moment the ships were out of sight, and beyond control from headquarters, their bows would be turned to some one or other of his recently acquired possessions, and that the contest for Africa, happily delayed for nearly four centuries, was about to be precipitated.

It would have been too much to expect that all difficulties had come to an end with the final clearance from land, as a crew so discontented at the start was sure to grow mutinous before the finish. Ere the squadron had proceeded far upon the open sea, the *Pinta* became suddenly disabled, and there was more than a suspicion that the damage was wilful, and inflicted by some of the sailors at the direct instigation of the owners, who hoped by that means to procure her return. The admiral, however, was not to be disconcerted much less turned from his purpose by a trivial detail like that; and as, fortunately, the Canary Islands were still ahead, they made for them in order that, if possible, a new vessel might be procured. That being impracticable, the *Pinta* was hastily repaired, causing a delay of some three weeks; and all the would-be scuttlers earned for their pains was that they had to sail in a ship somewhat less seaworthy than before, though she still remained the fastest of the three. As strict injunctions had been given to each captain never to lose sight of the other vessels, the sailing capacities had of course to be regulated in accordance with the slowest; and fear, if no worthier motive, caused the order for a long time to be obeyed. Quicker progress was made, however, than most of the men had any idea of, and not even the pilots were taken into the confidence of Columbus, who was keeping two separate logs, in one of which he faithfully recorded the exact distance covered each day, together with every observation he had to make; while the other, for immediate publication, minimised the number of leagues sailed, and deceived the crews as to their real distance from home.

That became more and more necessary as day after day passed, and all that met the strained and anxious gaze was a boundless waste of water. The weather continued favourable, and few difficulties of navigation were encountered, the only real cause for alarm being a variation of the compasses, such as the oldest and most experienced seaman had neither experienced nor heard of, and as to the reason for which Columbus had to hazard a guess, and express it as an ascertained fact in order to allay uneasiness. This was not the main cause of anxiety, however. The ships were sailing in an unknown sea; the very ease with which they moved forward might prove an impediment to their return (there was, of course, no knowledge then that the current as well as the prevailing winds favoured navigation from west to east rather than from east to west); and even at the artificial computation, they were farther away from home than the most desponding had ever ventured to imagine possible without certain disaster, but this, so far from reassuring them, only led them to conjure up fresh terrors. Demands to reverse the course grew louder and more persistent; and had not the Pinzons remained loyal to their admiral, and overawed their crews, no power on earth would have induced the latter to allow Columbus to proceed. He himself was surprised that land had not been made earlier, as he had reckoned Japan to be much nearer. How astonished he would have been to learn, when success had crowned his efforts, that he was still but a third of the distance he imagined he had covered! He subdued the murmurs, therefore, by undertaking that if, within a given period, no land were sighted or encouragement forthcoming, he would return. Not that he entertained the slightest intention of abandoning the enterprise, but there had been signs which convinced him that the goal was near. False ones, it is true, for they were merely land birds; but ornithology had then revealed little or nothing about migration; and the most diligent student of natural history would have been dumfounded at the very notion of the flights regularly undertaken at each returning season.

As this occurred on the 14th September, no great length of time had elapsed since the commencement of the voyage, allowance being made for the delay at the Canaries. But in those days it was something quite unusual to lose sight of land at all, and a few weeks upon the open sea appeared an eternity. Even the few bolder spirits who had voluntarily embarked in the enterprise, began to despair; and as Columbus would not return, they endeavoured to persuade him to deviate the course, and set the helms either for a more northerly or more southerly direction. He persisted, however, in making due west, and exhibited all the stubbornness on the quarter-deck that had been so marked a feature of his character while at the Courts of Portugal and Spain.

On the 25th September, all the labour and anxiety of the previous seven or eight weeks appeared as though it had met with its reward, and amid universal rejoicing Martin Pinzon reported that he had descried land to the south-west. But it turned out to be as great a delusion as the evidence afforded by the birds, or the vast area of weeds through which it had occupied the vessels several days in slowly forcing their way. Such false reports were not at all unlikely, as Columbus, having promised a handsome donation to the first man who should descry land, all on board were naturally eager to gain it, and every cloud on the horizon would be pointed out as the possible realisation of the hope. One distinct advantage, at anyrate, was secured, by giving the men something else than their grievances to think about.

Nearly a month had elapsed since the sighting of the land birds, and still no sign anywhere of solid ground. At last, unmistakable evidence of its proximity was afforded. A branch of thorn bearing red berries was seen floating on the bosom of the waters. Then a rudely carved staff, and detached weeds, such as were known to grow only in fresh river water. Orders were given that the three vessels should lay-to at night, lest land should be passed in the darkness, or, worse still, collision with it should result in disaster. While in this condition, Columbus, on the night of the 12th October, descried in the distance an unsteady light, as though shed from a lantern waved about or carried from one place to another, and though only exhibited for a brief period, it was distinctly observed by several others whose attention was directed to it. Morning light was eagerly awaited, and as the dawn broke, there sure enough lay the consummation of their hopes! To Columbus himself was allotted the promised reward, though it was claimed by a seaman who had previously pointed out certain indications in the exact quarter in which the first island was discovered, and to whom, under the circumstances, it would have been politic to award it.

There was a remarkable absence of exciting incident in this voyage of seventy days, fraught with such immense consequences to the whole world. Though made at a period of the year when the Atlantic is usually visited by the equinoctial disturbances, no unduly severe weather was encountered; and a belief was even indulged in, that these distant waters were outside the sphere of storms, until some very bitter experiences proved the contrary. What was accomplished by design, however, in 1492, would have been revealed by accident only eight years later, when a Portuguese captain, Pedro Alvarez Cabral by name, on his voyage to the East, was driven so far out of his course by storms, that he touched the coast of Brazil. Spain, therefore, became the mistress of the New World, not only by the skin of its teeth, but by a stupendous error in calculation; for though Columbus had rightly judged the shape of the earth, he so far underestimated its immensity, as to believe that the farthest East lay within easy reach of the West. Nor was the mistake discovered until many years later, and in the meantime the appellation of the Indies was assigned to the newly revealed territory, with the subsequent prefix of West to distinguish it from the real Indies, when these were proved beyond doubt to lie at the opposite quarter of the globe.

## III

## ACQUISITION

THE discovery proved no barren one. Not only was there land, but the inhabitants crowded down to the beach to stare at the immense floating objects with wings, the like of which they had never before seen. Would they receive the Spaniards as friends, or oppose them stoutly as foes? was the question that presented itself at once to the mind of Columbus; and in making preparations for landing, he not only saw that the force which was to accompany him was well-armed, but likewise well-habited, in order that a feeling of awe might be instilled into the minds of the natives.

These precautions proved entirely unnecessary, for the most striking feature of the new-comers was their white skins; and this, together with the manner of their arrival, raised them at once to the dignity of deities descended from the heavens. It soon became evident from the display of simplicity, as well as of apparent ignorance, that these could not be the people spoken of by Marco Polo and other Eastern travellers; and the conclusion was formed by Columbus and his more intelligent followers, that they had touched at some outlying territory, and that Zipangu and Cathay lay still farther west. Difficult as communication was between peoples absolutely ignorant of each other's language, the Spaniards, with their preconceived notions, soon gained sufficient information to confirm them in this idea; and as the little island of San Salvador, as it was named, the Watling Island of to-day, was quickly found to be altogether too small to afford facilities for colonisation, little time was lost in making a fresh start. Columbus, however, in his brief intercourse with the natives, had fully reciprocated their friendly spirit, and so ingratiated himself with them that, without much difficulty, he prevailed upon seven to accompany him on board his vessel, with the object principally of being instructed in the Castilian tongue, and thus making themselves useful as interpreters.

Sailing in the direction designated, where, as was supposed, lay the territories of the Grand Khan, the vessels touched in quick succession at several of the islands of the Lucayos, or Bahamas group, but none were any more inviting for permanent residence than San Salvador. Everywhere, indeed, there was tropical profusion, and men might subsist by the mere labour entailed in gathering the natural fruits of the earth; but gold was now the one thing sought, as its existence in these regions was beyond dispute, from the small ornaments already obtained from the natives in exchange for hawks' bells, glass beads, and other such like trinkets. Of commercial instinct these simple creatures had not a trace, and they would have given everything they possessed for the most worthless trifle, provided it was a novelty, had not Columbus restrained their liberality, and forbidden his followers to take undue advantage of it. His aim was to discover the source of this golden wealth ere he returned home, and no one was more anxious than he to accumulate a solid trophy of his much ridiculed expedition; but, entirely apart from his humane and generous disposition, he clearly realised that future success depended to a very large extent upon the continued friendly and trustful disposition of the new subjects of the Castilian Crown. For such they were the moment they came into contact with Columbus, whose first care was to take formal possession, on behalf of Queen Isabella, of every inch of territory embraced by the islands on which he landed.

On the 28th October, sixteen days after the first discovery, the coast of Cuba hove in sight. As an impression prevailed that this at last was the mainland, an embassy was despatched into the interior to notify the mighty potentate supposed to rule over that vast continent, of the arrival of the representative of the Spanish sovereigns, who were desirous of entering into close relationship with him. Needless to say, the mission was fruitless; and the members of it soon became convinced that they were altogether on the wrong tack, as nowhere did they meet with any sign of civilisation, and scarcely anywhere of population. From what little information they were able to glean, the land of promise was still somewhat farther south.

Martin Alonso Pinzon had been quietly noting all he heard, and being in command of the fastest caravel, the *Pinta*, he determined to profit by it, and forestall his admiral, not only in arriving first at the place where gold was so abundant, but also in conveying the marvellous news to Spain. With this object in view, he deserted on the 21st November, but his plans miscarried, and Columbus fell in with him at a later date after his own vessel, the *Santa Maria*, had been totally wrecked on a sandbank off the coast of Hayti. That island was reached on the 6th December, and gave more evidence of being the place they were in search of than any they had yet touched. It was populous, gold was much more abundant, and the natives made it clear that it was to be found in large quantities in the interior. Several circumstances made it advisable for Columbus to return to Spain without further delay. He had seen enough to be convinced that a much larger force than he had under his command would be necessary to make the subjugation of these newly acquired territories effective; news of the discovery might reach Europe before him, and be taken advantage of by some other sovereign than the one to whom he was devoted; and he had now sufficient treasure of various kinds to convince the most sceptical of the complete success of his enterprise. After constructing a small fort out of the materials of the wreck, and leaving a portion of the crew, at their own desire, to garrison it until he should return, he set sail for home with the *Niña* on the 4th January 1493. Falling in with Pinzon, who had experienced nothing but ill-luck since his desertion, the two ships finally cleared the island a few days later.

The return voyage was as full of peril as the outward one had been free from it. Indeed, at one time, it looked as though the prognostications of the people of Palos would be fulfilled, and no living soul return to his native land. That two such battered wrecks ever survived the storms they encountered, can only be attributed to the direct intervention of Providence. Columbus, in the full conviction that nothing could save them, prepared a record of the voyage, sealed it, with outward instructions that if ever found it was to be conveyed to the Court of Spain, and having placed it in a barrel made water-tight, committed it to the waves. As there is no record of it ever having been picked up, the story of

# ACQUISITION

the discovery of America, as we know it, would never have been written, had not Columbus survived to tell it.

He was only too delighted to find himself at last off the Azores, though, being a Portuguese possession, he would not in the ordinary course have dreamt of calling at them. As it was, he ran considerable risk from the perfidy of the governor, and was glad to escape without repairing any of the damage to his ships. Subsequent stress of weather compelled him to make for and put in at Lisbon, where his arrival created intense excitement, and King John learned what he had lost by his refusal to listen to the projects of the great discoverer. Many of his subjects urged that it was even then not too late, that Columbus and his crew might be prevented from returning to Spain, and that an expedition might be immediately fitted out to cross the sea and enter into possession of the territories beyond. John, however, was too magnanimous to listen to such proposals, and not only accorded his former suppliant a hearty welcome and brilliant reception, but afforded him the protection necessary to enable him to reach home.

If the excitement at Lisbon was great, what must it have been at Palos, when the solitary *Niña* arrived on the 13th March, the *Pinta* having again deserted, arriving only some days later! The news spread with lightning rapidity, and we may be sure lost nothing of its weight and importance as it winged its way. Columbus was summoned to Barcelona, where Ferdinand and Isabella were then domiciled, made a triumphal entry into the city, and on his arrival at the royal residence, was welcomed by the king and queen in person, who commanded him to be seated by their side, while he related the account of his adventures.

The first thing to be done was to secure the fruits of this marvellous venture. Portugal sought to protect its possessions, not only by force of arms, but by taking advantage of the fiction that all heathen countries were in the gift of the Pope, and had obtained from him a Bull confirming its rights. Spain immediately followed suit, and as the then occupant of the chair of St. Peter, Alexander VI., was himself a Spaniard, a refusal was hardly likely, though the notorious Roderigo Borgia was far more actuated by self-interest than any patriotic feelings. The Bull confirmed the Portuguese in their existing possessions, and granted them all territory that should be discovered east of a line drawn from north to south, one hundred leagues west of the Azores, while the Spaniards were to enjoy exclusive dominion over everything west of it.

This was regarded as so unsatisfactory by Portugal, that at its instigation, negotiations between the two countries were opened, and resulted the following year in the conclusion of the Treaty of Tordesillas, by which it was agreed to move the line 370 leagues west of the Azores, a most important change, because by it Portugal subsequently established its claim to the Brazils, a portion of which was found to fall east of the line of demarcation, while it could urge the further plea of having been first in the field, through the accidental deviation of Cabral. At anyrate, the whole world outside Europe was leased in perpetuity to Spain and Portugal; and had the pretensions of the Holy See in things temporal as well as spiritual continued to be recognised, neither England, France, nor Germany could to-day own a square yard of territory in the three greatest continents of the world.

While these negotiations were in progress, preparations for a second expedition on a vastly greater scale were rapidly pushed forward. The direction of them was entrusted to a cleric named Fonseca, a capable man of business, but who for some reason or other conceived a violent dislike to Columbus, and threw every obstacle in his way. The eagerness to embark on this second voyage was far more marked than the reluctance exhibited in the first, and the best blood of Spain pressed into the service. The number of adventurers was originally limited to a thousand; but the applications were so numerous from those who believed that fortunes were waiting to be picked up in the New World, that this was raised to twelve hundred, and fifteen hundred actually sailed in seventeen vessels from the Bay of Cadiz on the 25th September 1493.

All was keen anticipation during the voyage, the disappointments only commenced at its termination. Into these there is no occasion to enter now. The main point of interest is, that a sufficiently large force of Spaniards had taken part in the enterprise to confirm the possession of the New World to their country, and defeat any attempts that Portugal might be likely to make to filch it away. After establishing a settlement at Isabella on the north of Hayti, or Hispaniola as it was then named, Columbus was free to prosecute further explorations, the principal one being to sail along the southern shores of Cuba; but, after continuing his voyage to within a few miles of its western extremity, he arrived at the conclusion that it was the mainland, and reported to that effect—nor was it until after his death that it was proved to be an island. Everything was claimed for the Spanish Crown; and, as there were absolutely no competitors, it can well be understood how the entire group of islands constituting the West Indies became Spanish colonies.

Various causes compelled Columbus to relinquish his exploration and return, first to Hispaniola and then to Spain. For one thing, the two vessels with which he set sail were ill-provisioned. With that confidence in his own judgment which was so characteristic of the man, he relied upon encountering at no great distance those civilised, or at least, semi-civilised nations of which he had come in search, but instead he met only the fierce tribes of Cuba and Jamacia, who offered resistance, not welcome, and arrows in lieu of food.

On his return to the colony, affairs were in a most unsatisfactory condition. The last thing most of the colonists dreamt of when they left their native shores was work. They had gone out, as they fondly imagined, to pick up the gold as it lay at their feet, and when they had accumulated sufficient, meant to return and enjoy it. Though Columbus had never promised, nor even suggested anything of the sort, his brilliant descriptions and anticipations were undoubtedly responsible for the ideas so freely indulged, and the indignation against him rose just as rapidly as hopes were blasted. Complaints were finding their way to Spain, and lest he should be prejudiced in the eyes of his sovereigns, he determined to embark thence and render a personal account of his stewardship.

The voyage home was if anything more protracted, and entailed greater hardships than the previous one. Columbus arrived at Cadiz on the 1st June 1496, and met with a warmer reception than he had dared to hope for. But intrigue was busy, and his arch-enemy Fonseca, who was by this time in almost undisputed control of

## ACQUISITION

colonial affairs, threw numerous and persistent obstacles in the way of his fitting out another expedition. The stories told by returned colonists of the want and suffering they had endured were not conducive to others volunteering for the service, and it was only on the 30th May 1498 that the admiral was again able to set sail from San Lucar with a small fleet of six vessels, manned almost entirely by convicts specially released.

A more southerly course was taken than on either of the previous occasions, and the first place touched was the island of Trinidad. Sailing round it from the southwest, the ships were suddenly caught and swept along by a mighty current, which Columbus discovered to be of fresh water, and rightly judged to be poured out of some vast river. He had in fact reached the coast of South America, and was in the waters of the Orinoco as they rushed to mingle with the ocean. The natives proved of a more friendly disposition, as well as of superior type to those encountered in many of the islands; and as they possessed gold, and also something still more precious, pearls, every encouragement was given them to trade. They were just as eager after the trumpery toys of the Old World, as the inhabitants of San Salvador had been the first time they were ever exhibited in the New, and we may be sure the bargains made were very profitable to the Spaniards. Still, these were not the people Columbus had come in search of, and his inquiries and labours were diligently directed to the discovery of a passage which should lead him still farther west to the dominions of the Grand Khan.

After some time vainly spent in exploring the coast with this object, an affection of the eyes compelled him to desist and make once more for Hispaniola, where he had left his brother Bartholomew as governor during his absence. A strange welcome awaited him, however. In response to the continued complaints of the colonists, a commissioner had been despatched from Spain to inquire into their grievances, and certain powers were entrusted to him to assume authority in the island in case of necessity. Deeply impressed with a sense of his own importance, Francisco Bobadilla, the officer appointed, immediately on his arrival began to act in the most reckless and arbitrary manner; and the discoverer of the New World, without any warning, found himself arrested, loaded with chains, thrown into prison, and finally sent home to Spain in this ignominious fashion.

Great was the public, still greater the royal indignation, when he arrived in this sorry plight; every effort was made to soothe the feelings so deeply wounded by this dire insult, and Bobadilla would have paid dearly for his temerity had he survived to answer for his misdeeds. But news had reached Spain of the wonderful riches of the Gulf of Paria some time before the arrival of Columbus, and the malignant and untiring Fonseca, in direct contravention of the charter conveying the rights to the admiral, stimulated private enterprise to follow in the track, taking the utmost possible advantage of whatever information he had gained in his official capacity, and imparting it to others. An expedition was fitted out under Alonso de Ojeda, one of the most dare-devil adventurers who ever quitted the shores of his own or any other country, and whose marvellous exploits in Hispaniola had already excited the wonder and admiration of men long accustomed to feats of skill and courage. Accompanying him was Amerigo Vespucci, a Venetian navigator, who

## ACQUISITION

strangely enough was destined to give his name to the whole of the vast Continent which he was about to visit for the first time, though he never accomplished anything of practical importance in it. Several other ships were fitted out, including a caravel of 50 tons burden by Pedro Alonso Niño, which performed the most lucrative voyage of any vessel or squadron equipped up to that time, and returned home well freighted with pearls and other costly treasure. This was quite sufficient to stimulate ambition as well as greed, and when Columbus arrived he had the mortification of learning that others were actively exploiting his preserves.

While these events were happening, another enterprise was undertaken quite beyond the cognisance of the Spanish authorities. Bartholomew Columbus, it will be remembered, had proceeded on a mission to Henry VII. some years previous ; and when the English monarch learned that the most sanguine anticipations had been realised, he was anxious to share in the results. As early as 1495 he endeavoured to equip and despatch a squadron of his own, but it was not until two years later that Sebastian Cabot, despite the existence of the Papal Bull, set sail from Bristol. Steering a direct westerly course, he struck the coast of Newfoundland, and leisurely sailed south almost to the extreme point of Florida, ere he resumed his homeward journey. The Spanish Government naturally protested against this infringement of its rights, and Henry found it politic to listen, as he was then in close alliance, and engaged in negotiating the marriage between his son and Catherine of Aragon, which subsequently proved so pregnant to the religious and ecclesiastical destinies of England. It was at a later period, and under totally different circumstances, that the Anglo-Saxon race was to occupy and overrun the northern continent.

Columbus himself was spared to undertake one more voyage, and this time it was to be confined exclusively to the continent, he being absolutely forbidden to land at Hispaniola, where Nicolas Ovando, with a force of all sorts and conditions of men numbering 2500 had been installed as governor, and so jealous was he of any interference with his prerogatives, that when the admiral was driven by stress of weather to take shelter in the harbour of San Domingo, he was ordered to quit instantly.

This proved the most disastrous of all his voyages. After exploring the coasts of Honduras and Central America generally, in search of the non-existent channel, until the provisions were in such a state that they could only be eaten in the dark, it was decided to land, despite the fierce opposition of the natives, and plant a permanent settlement under Bartholomew, who accompanied his brother. This, however, had to be abandoned; and on the way back the only remaining vessel ran aground in Dry Harbour in Jamaica, and became a total wreck, the most incredible suffering, aggravated by constant mutiny, being experienced, until the remnant of the crew was eventually relieved.

Columbus having shown the way to the mainland, as well as the islands, it was left to others to reveal the vast extent and natural wealth of what he had discovered, and he died on the 20th May 1506, in complete ignorance of many of the most important facts which his genius and tenacity permitted to be made known for the first time to the civilised world.

Columbus and his immediate followers hit upon the

## ACQUISITION

most unpromising part of the American Continent, where the damp hot atmosphere, with its resulting rank and profuse vegetation, makes human existence intolerable if not well-nigh impossible. As the land was known to contain gold, however, the most persistent efforts were made to settle in it, and two regular governments were established under Alonso de Ojeda and Diego de Nicuessa respectively. Nothing but disaster resulted for many a long year, and the greatest difficulties were experienced in extending or enlarging them in any direction but coastwise.

Narrow as the isthmus is in the part selected, it appeared impenetrable, until eventually the magic word gold encouraged a few bold spirits to overcome every obstacle. Wherever the adventurers went inland they heard of a great sea and vast abundance of the precious metal in an unknown land beyond. After incredible hardships, Vasco Nuñez de Balboa and a handful of followers forced their way through the thickets and swamps, scaled the mountain range which runs like a backbone along the isthmus, and were rewarded for their pains when they reached the summit by the sight of the great southern sea lying at their feet. This occurred on the 26th September 1513, and on the following day the party descended the western slopes; Vasco Nuñez, as its leader and commander, taking possession of the Pacific Ocean on behalf of the King of Spain, with all the ceremonies and formalities customary on those occasions.

How to take advantage of it was the question? Far south, beyond where vision could reach, lay the golden land. They were without ships or means of conveyance of any sort, and the shore upon which they were now stranded was dangerous as well as inhospitable. The observant and ingenious mind of Nuñez, inferior only to that of Columbus, evolved the idea of transporting material across the isthmus for the construction of a fleet to undertake the subjugation of all countries bordering on the Southern Sea; and such was the work eventually accomplished, though not by Nuñez, who fell a victim to the jealousy and treachery of Pedrarias Davila, a new governor despatched from Spain. It was left to one of his lieutenants, Francisco Pizarro, to set forth on a definite expedition more than ten years later; and it was not until nearly twenty years had elapsed that Peru was discovered, and the rich kingdom of the Incas added to the spoils of the Castilian monarch.

Meanwhile, exploration had been busy on the eastern side of the continent. Cuba, realised at length to be an island, was regularly colonised in 1511, and the governor, Diego Velasquez, being an enterprising and ambitious man, despatched an expedition westwards. The great peninsula of Yucatan was reached, and the officers of the little squadron were struck by the much higher state of civilisation exhibited by the natives than by any others hitherto met with either in the islands or on the mainland. The news of this led to the subsequent expedition of Cortes, the story of whose conquest of Mexico reads more like a fairy tale, than the narrative of actual events and hard realities.

The years, 1519, 1520, and 1521, were occupied by this, the greatest of all the enterprises undertaken by Spain in the New World. Nor was there any lack of activity in other directions. Juan Ponce sailed from Porto Rico in 1512, in search of a spring whose waters ensured perennial youth to whoever drank of them, and found and annexed Florida instead. More than one navigator cruised southwards as far as the Rio de la Plata, and in 1520 Magellan reached the extremity of the southern continent, and passed through the straits which bear his name. Nor was Cortes idle after he had accomplished his great work. North and south he sought to add to the territory of New Spain, until all the countries of Central America on one side, and the peninsula of California on the other, were brought under its sway. In less than half a century from the day Columbus first set foot on San Salvador, the entire continent, from Labrador to Patagonia, had been visited, and by far the greater part of it annexed to, and nominally ruled by the Castilian Crown.

While Spain was actively engaged in exploration and annexation in the West, Portugal was equally busy in the East. Though the Cape of Good Hope had been doubled by Diaz in 1486, it was not until 1497, five years after the discovery of America, that Vasco de Gama proved the possibility of reaching India by that route. Rapid progress, for those days at anyrate, was made from that time. The actual neighbourhood of the Cape apparently offered no attractions; the advantages of its situation were left to be realised by the Dutch a century later; and it was not until Natal was reached on Christmas Day, whence its name, that there were any thoughts of annexation or settlement. It was the East Coast of Africa which seemed to offer the greatest facilities for communication and trading with the opposite shores of India, and claimed attention accordingly; and as numerous pilots were to be found there, skilled in navigating vessels across the Indian Ocean, it was there colonies were first established, one of which at least, and the only important one remaining to

Portugal, Lorenzo Marques, has been the object of envy, and the source of much contention in recent years. From the Malabar coast in the south to Karachi in the north of India, Portuguese traders grew active, but, owing to the fierceness and determination of the natives, it was found impossible for some years to permanently occupy any territory, until Goa was established in 1510, as the centre of Portuguese interests. A year earlier than this, Malacca had been subjugated, and the exploration of Sumatra undertaken ; while three years later, Francisco Serrão discovered the Moluccas, the far-famed islands from which Venice and Genoa had so long drawn their stores of valuable spices by the overland route through India and Persia, or by the Red Sea and Isthmus of Suez. To divert this traffic round the Cape of Good Hope, expeditions were fitted out against Muscat and Ormuz in the Persian Gulf, and Aden at the entrance to the Red Sea. While, then, the Spanish colonists were searching for gold in sufficient quantities to make the enterprise pay, much less realise fortunes, the Portuguese tapped the source of wealth of the great mercantile communities of the Middle Ages, and, monopolising it themselves, rendered their country for a time the richest in the world.

Of the numerous governors despatched by Portugal to the East, the Duke of Albuquerque was the most active, and accomplished the greatest results. Serving under him in various capacities was Ferrão Magalhaes, or Maghallanes, a young nobleman who sought on every possible occasion to distinguish himself. Returning home, he did not receive the reward he considered his due ; and though he continued to agitate at Court, and to urge his claims, on the further ground that since his arrival from the East he had taken part in an African campaign, and been permanently lamed, he was either repulsed or put off with some trifling concession. This rankling in his mind, he determined to divest himself of his nationality, and offer his services to Spain, the patron of all foreign adventurers.

By the Papal Bull, Spain was debarred from undertaking any enterprise in the East. This was, of course, well known to Magalhaes, or Ferdinand Magellan as he now chose to call himself, but he had carefully thought the matter out, and arrived at a conclusion of his own. He had heard much of the ideas which led to the discovery of America, and though other and more important matters then engaged the attention of Spain than the discovery of Japan and China by the western route, he still considered the plan feasible. He intimated to the Emperor Charles V., then King of Spain, his desire to be entrusted with an expedition, with which he would undertake to reach the Moluccas from the west, and so prove that they belonged by right to Spain.

News of this treachery reached Portugal, where it was heard with the greatest indignation, and an angry correspondence passed between the two Courts. Charles' ambitions, however, lay in European aggrandisement, for which the demands upon his exchequer were heavier than he well knew how to meet. His great possessions in the New World had hitherto been a drain upon his scanty resources, as they had been upon those of his grandfather before him ; and although Ferdinand lived for a quarter of a century after the discovery of America, he left hardly sufficient money in his coffers to pay his funeral expenses. Charles, therefore, listened eagerly to the proposition by which he might acquire the teeming riches of the Spice Islands, and, notwithstanding protests and warnings alike, terms were finally agreed to in March 1518, which placed five ships, and a full complement of men, at the disposal of Magellan. Failing any other means of putting an end to the enterprise, a plot was formed for the assassination of Magellan, but miscarried; and he weighed anchor on the 10th August 1519, though delayed in his actual departure until the 20th September following.

Instructions were sent to the Brazils, already occupied by Portugal, to waylay Magellan, and at all costs prevent the continuance of his voyage; and in case he eluded the vigilance of the governor of that settlement, a strict watch was to be kept at the Moluccas, and no quarter given him if he ever reached there, as he was declared a traitor to the Crown of Portugal. He arrived at the Rio de la Plata unmolested, and entered that river, of great width at its mouth and for some distance along its course, with the idea that it offered the long sought passage to the West. The increasing freshness of the water convinced him that it was but a river, and he returned and moved his course southwards. And now his real difficulties began. Winter was setting in with all its rigour, and the farther south he proceeded the more severe became the weather. His crew was most cosmopolitan in character and nationality, and included a number of Portuguese, some of whom, it began to be suspected, had been bribed to mutiny, if not indeed to murder their commander. Dissensions broke out amongst the captains of the different vessels on petty points of precedence and discipline; and only the most determined stand by Magellan himself, who did not hesitate to hang several of the crew as an example to the rest, prevented the total ruin of his hopes and plans.

To make matters worse, scarcity of provisions began to be experienced, and it was then decided to winter in the shelter of the river St. Julian. It was in October 1520 before a fresh start could be made, and on the 21st of that month a channel was discovered, the careful navigation of which for thirty-eight days, amid shoals and innumerable islands, brought them, amid great rejoicing, once more into the open sea, proving the theory maintained by Columbus to his dying day to be so far, at anyrate, correct.

But Magellan, like all his predecessors, sadly miscalculated the distance between the remote East and the far West, and after taking in such supplies of provisions as were obtainable, renewed his voyage with a light heart, and in full expectation of reaching land in a week or two at longest. Days grew into weeks, and the weeks passed into months, and still no break on the monotonous horizon. The sufferings of the crew were horrible, as food and water became gradually exhausted, and they had to subsist at last by gnawing anything into which they could get their teeth. To turn back was certain destruction, as they could not possibly last out the time necessary to cover the distance already traversed. To go forward, therefore, was their only chance of salvation; and after a passage of ninety-eight days, land was sighted on the 18th March, and the most dreaded of their dangers passed. They had sailed into a group of islands, not the Moluccas as they had anticipated, but the Islas de las Pintados, so called from the custom of the natives of painting or tattooing their naked bodies, and subsequently re-christened the Philippines, in honour of the heir to the Spanish throne, who afterwards reigned as Philip II.

Magellan was not destined to reap the fruits of his

enterprise, nor to suffer the punishment subsequently inflicted on some of the survivors. He found the natives among whom he first landed friendly disposed, but rightly suspected them of treachery. Desirous, however, of conciliating them as far as possible, he entered into their quarrel with a tribe in a neighbouring island, and, in the attack which he led against it, was slain. Disputes arose as to who should succeed to the command; and what was left of the fleet, after many adventures and the loss of a considerable number of the crew, arrived at the island of Tidor in the Moluccas on the 8th November 1521. There it was decided that the *Victoria* should load a cargo of spices and make its way to Spain by the Cape of Good Hope, in direct defiance of the rights of the Portuguese, while the *Trinidad* should return the way she came. A valuable cargo, consisting of about twenty-six tons of cloves, with parcels of cinnamon, sandal wood, and nutmegs, was shipped, and after being nearly captured by the Portuguese off the African coast, and again at the Canaries, arrived in the harbour of San Lucar, as was supposed, on the 6th September 1522, having sailed round the world in three years all but a few days. Through all their troubles, a careful record of dates had been kept, and the officers were surprised to find that what they imagined to be the 6th was actually the 7th September in Seville; and they were at a loss to know how the one day had been missed, being of course unaware that this is the invariable result of circumnavigating the world from East to West.

Of the total number of 280 hands originally shipped, only a remnant remained, of whom seventeen, together with the captain, Juan Sebastian Elcano, were on board the *Victoria*. They were received with great rejoicing, and Charles conferred a pension of 500 ducats on

## ACQUISITION

Elcano; but what fate would have awaited Magellan is doubtful, as the captain and crew of the *San Antonio*, which had deserted in the Straits on the outward voyage, were cast into prison, and the most hostile reports had been spread as to the misconduct and tyranny of the admiral of the squadron.

Proof was thus afforded of the possibility of reaching the Spice Islands by a westerly route, and Charles was not the sovereign to relinquish the rights which he supposed this conferred upon him. He realised, however, that whatever connection he maintained with them, must be from the West and not from the East; and accordingly the second expedition set out by the same route, but in the meantime orders were sent by the Portuguese to strongly fortify the Moluccas. The continental engagements of Charles, together with the absorbing claims of America, caused the East Indies for a time to be neglected, the discoveries of gold having by this time become of greater consequence than the slow accumulation of spices. Urgently in need of money, the Emperor in 1529, in consideration of a loan of 350,000 ducats from the King of Portugal, agreed to cede whatever rights he possessed in these islands; and when the third expedition was planned in 1542 from Mexico, it was directed solely to the Philippines, and express injunctions given not to interfere in any way with the Moluccas.

It was not until 1564 that any definite attempt was made at annexation. Again the voyage was undertaken from Mexico, this time under Miguel Lopez de Legaspi, who landed at Cebu on the 27th April 1565, and formally took possession. He remained as governor, and five years later his grandson set sail for Luzon, the largest island of the group, which numbers, in all some six hundred, and having captured the capital, fortified it and made Manila the centre of government. A municipal council was constituted the following year, and Spain has retained possession of the islands ever since, though not without her rights being more than once seriously contested. In 1574 a Chinese pirate, Lama-hong, long a terror in Eastern waters, arrived off Manila with sixty-two junks and a large force of fighting-men, and was with difficulty repulsed; while in 1762 the British actually captured the capital, and would probably have overrun the entire island, had not the Treaty of Paris the following year terminated hostilities between Great Britain and Spain.

For a lengthy period there was no direct connection with the mother country, and the Philippines were embraced in the viceroyalty of New Spain, through which the whole of its commerce passed. A galleon sailed once a year from Acapulco to Manila, carrying bullion for the purchase of merchandise, as well as for the necessities of the Government, together with such manufactures as found a sale there, and took back in exchange the products of the colony, which in due course were conveyed across the isthmus to Porto Bello, and shipped to Europe, a roundabout way which could not survive the demands and competition of modern commerce. The loss of Mexico did not entail the forfeiture of the Eastern possessions, as the revolting Mexicans had no desire to burden themselves with such distant responsibilities. Outbreaks in the islands themselves have been numerous, but always hitherto suppressed. It remains to be seen whether Spain can much longer maintain a hold over the Philippines, any more than over the last of its once great American possessions.

## IV

## EXPLOITATION

HOWEVER desirous Columbus may have been to impart the truths of Christianity to the benighted denizens of the East, there can be no denying the fact that he never lost sight of the main chance of the material benefit likely to accrue from his voyages and discoveries. It was his demand for a tenth of all revenues to be derived from territories he might annex to the Castilian Crown, as well as the hereditary governorship, that so nearly lost Spain the temporary ownership of the New World, though that should hardly have stood in the way with men who believed the enterprise would prove valueless, if not disastrous. Of the entire crew who accompanied him on his first voyage, scarce a dozen anticipated any gain to themselves or anyone else, and we can imagine the feelings of delight, therefore, with which they first viewed the little golden ornaments worn by the natives of San Salvador. A vista of possibilities at once opened up before them. From dreams of a watery grave or a bottomless abyss, they were suddenly transported to the realities of an unknown land, which they promptly persuaded themselves was teeming with wealth; and wealth in those days had only one meaning—gold.

When the island of Hayti spread itself out before them, with its evident large population, from which they received a most hearty welcome, and its promise of abundant sustenance, it is hardly surprising that many of the men who left their native shores with such reluctance, were equally chary to return. Columbus himself was only too ready to fall in with their views, and hoped that during the somewhat prolonged absence which his voyage home and back again would necessarily entail, the little colony he was about to plant at Navidad would use all diligence in exploring the interior, so that by the time he returned with a greatly increased force, everything would be ready for the systematic development of this fine estate.

The admiral was the one man who retained a clear head amid all the excitement. He foresaw that events might arise which would speedily convert the natives from friends to foes, and out of the materials of the wreck of the *Santa Maria*, which lay close at hand, he caused a fort to be constructed; and despicable as it must have appeared in the eyes of a European soldier, it was thought to be amply strong enough to afford protection against an unwarlike tribe, possessed of no weapons, and, as far as could be judged, utterly devoid of military skill. The greatest protection of all, however, must be to dwell on intimate terms with those by whom they were surrounded, and to avoid every cause of offence; and these were the strict injunctions given by Columbus at his departure. The true history of that colony will never be known, as, when the second expedition arrived, not a living soul was left to relate it. All that could be gathered concerning it had to be collected from native sources, which varied somewhat; but it was only too evident that, when the restraining hand of their captain was removed, the indulgence of every desire and passion was permitted to run riot; and a terrible

# EXPLOITATION

revenge was taken, not by the tribe amongst whom they actually dwelt, but by another and fiercer one from the interior with which somehow or other they came into contact. How often since has this sad story been repeated, either in whole or in part!

This disaster to a handful of their fellow-countrymen was not likely to deter the crowd, which now for the first time came out to exploit the riches of the New World. To begin with, all was energy and enthusiasm, but the ardour soon began to cool, and ere long gave way to positive despair. The source of the gold which was to have been at least discovered, if not actually opened up and ready for work, was still unknown, and lay somewhere in the interior defended by fierce barbarians. The food supplies began to run out; the natives, extremely frugal in their diet, as all the gentler inhabitants of the tropics are, had sufficient for themselves, and to spare for a few chance visitors; but it became a serious matter to have to provide for fifteen hundred hungry intruders, the capacities of whose stomachs was not their least surprising characteristic in the minds of their hosts. In addition, there was no adequate shelter for such a large company, which soon began to experience the inconveniences of tropical rains and hurricanes. Columbus, with his usual commonsense, perceived that the first thing to be done was the foundation of a settlement which should develop in due course into a city. A suitable site was chosen, and the town of Isabella built. But that was not the sort of work so many grandees of Spain had left the Old World to undertake; and as Columbus refused to recognise any distinctions of rank, and compelled all alike to bear their share of the necessary burdens, murmurs grew into discontent, and discontent ripened into rebellion. Thus early were planted the seeds of that spirit of turmoil and revolution which is still one of the leading features of every country and people which owe their origin to Spanish settlement, and which, despite full independence and occasional epochs of settled government, it seems utterly impossible to eradicate.

The mind of every reader must be prepared for all that followed. The maxims of Columbus were cast to the winds, his foreign birth was suddenly remembered against him as a crime, and the cry went up as of old, "We will not have this man to reign over us." Why should Spaniards work when there were natives to do it for them? was the first idea that struck them, and they became utterly heedless of the circumstance that the labour of the Indians in providing for their own wants was always of the lightest, and that toil in the European sense was unknown to them. The reward of their past faithfulness was compulsory service as hewers of wood and drawers of water, and in a very short time the entire population threatened to be reduced to a state of abject slavery.

Nor was Columbus himself entirely free from blame for the tendency which things were taking. In the second voyage, the fierce Caribs had been encountered in the islands south of Hayti, and had given every evidence of their cannibal propensities. The admiral, therefore, hoped at one stroke, by shipping to Spain as many as he could capture, to rid the neighbourhood of their unwelcome presence, to supply Spain itself with cheap labour such as Portugal drew from its African dominions, and to raise funds by their sale for the more rapid development of Hispaniola and the neighbouring islands, and thus allay, in part at least, the disappointment arising from the absence of gold in the quantities so confidently reckoned upon.

But the humanity and generous nature of Queen Isabella would not tolerate this degradation of the race, and her anger was roused even against her favourite. With her death, the unfortunate Indians lost, not perhaps their most ardent advocate — for the good, though in some points mistaken Las Casas must always occupy that honourable position — but certainly their most powerful protector; and though slavery in its most odious aspect was never tolerated, the increasing burdens and cruelties imposed on the natives, despite every edict of the Home Government to the contrary, rapidly diminished, until it almost exterminated them. Their places were taken by the African negro, who was found to be so much more hardy and enduring that one was counted equal to at least four Indians; and the trade, as is well known, grew with all its attendant horrors to enormous proportions. Perhaps the strangest thing about it is, that it was encouraged by the very people who took the Indians under their special protection, in the hope of thus relieving them; and in the attempt to remedy an evil and redress a wrong, a still greater one was perpetrated.

The rapid exhaustion of Hispaniola, even more than the love of adventure and excitement, was the cause of the creation of colonies elsewhere. That of course would not have been so, had not the inordinate thirst for gold led to the neglect of agriculture and every useful industry, for what for some time was but the pursuit of a will o' the wisp. Still, the most sanguine anticipations, even in this respect, were destined at no distant period to be more than fulfilled. The pearl fisheries, first at Paria, and then in the islands of the Pacific, opened up an unexpected source of wealth; but it was not until Montezuma offered his munificent gifts to Cortes, to induce the latter to quit the shores of Mexico, that the first great reservoir of the precious metals was tapped. Still, it must be remembered that the great stores of gold discovered, first in Mexico, and subsequently in Peru, did not in themselves imply that these countries were capable of continuing to produce unlimited quantities. They were the accumulations of many years, possibly of many centuries; for, as there was no foreign trade, everything produced which could not be consumed had necessarily to be preserved or destroyed.

It may be wondered what value gold possessed in the ideas of these people. That it was held in nothing like the same esteem as by Europeans is certain; but in Peru, at anyrate, its production and preservation were assured, from the fact that it was regarded as tears wept by the sun, which was the god of the people, whose Incas, or rulers, were called the Children of the Sun. In neither case, then, is it surprising that the treasure was not clung to with more tenacity. Both Montezuma and Atahualpa set a higher value upon many other things; and the quantities seized by Cortes and Pizarro and their respective followers, vast though it appeared in their eyes, and as it really was in those days, was parted with, with scarcely a pang of regret. That secured by Pizarro was by far the greater spoil, and was supposed to be the price of the freedom of the Inca himself, who offered to fill a room 35 feet by 17, and as high as a man could reach, with gold plate in exchange for it. He did not quite succeed, because Pizarro treacherously put him to death before the task was completed, yet the amount realised for distribution was equivalent to something like 3½ millions sterling of the money of to-day, and enriched the commonest foot-soldier beyond the dreams of avarice.

It was silver, not gold moreover, which eventually made both countries at once the wonder and the envy of the civilised world. The richest mines were unknown to the Indians, having only been discovered after the Spanish conquest. Those of Zacotecas in Mexico were first worked in 1532, while the more famous Potosi lode in Peru was laid bare in 1545, by a native scrambling up the side of a mountain in pursuit of some llamas which had strayed from his flock, and uprooting the shrubs to which he clung for support.

Desirous as the Spanish authorities at home were to obtain all the gold and silver possible, they were not blind to the fact, in the early days of colonisation at anyrate, that true success could only be ensured by permanent settlement. Columbus openly deplored the class of adventurers who sailed forth, and earnestly begged for sober and hard-working men. As governor-general of Hispaniola, he declined to make any grants of land except to those who had cultivated it for at least three years ; and the Government held out inducements with the same object, offering free passages, a supply of seed and live stock, and exemption from taxation on land and all agricultural produce. Among the 2500 souls accompanying Nicolas de Ovando in 1502, were seventy-three married men with their wives and families, and these formed the nucleus of the planting community that gradually sprang up. Ovando himself, though a bitter enemy of the Columbus family, adopted many of the principles laid down by its head, and specially encouraged the cultivation of the sugar-cane, which subsequently became the staple industry of the West Indies.

It goes without saying, that when the personal rights of the natives were so totally disregarded, their territorial ones were never so much as thought of; and a colonist had only to express a desire for lands, not in the occupation of a fellow-Spaniard, to receive them without question as to any other claim over them. The estates granted in this manner, particularly on the mainland, were often of immense area, and more like provinces or even kingdoms, while with these *encomiendas* as they were termed, went *repartimientos*, that is, allotments of Indians to cultivate them. Just as these had attained a higher grade of civilisation than their brethren on the islands, so were they capable of greater exertion, and negro slavery did not become so rife. But the demands upon their strength nevertheless proved excessive, and the mortality among them was so great as to threaten their extinction. That has not occurred, and their descendants, in greatly reduced numbers it is true, help to people South and Central America to-day.

But work in the mines deteriorated their physique, while the produce ruined the morals of their masters. Up to the end of last century, when Spain began to lose its hold over its South American possessions, the recorded import thence of gold and silver alone, considerably exceeded one thousand millions sterling; while good authorities calculate that quite as much more, some indeed say twice as much, was clandestinely sent to Europe to avoid the payment of duty. Could anything prove more conclusively that the precious metals are not the true source of wealth? Spain to-day is the poorest country in Europe, and tottering on the verge of bankruptcy.

## V

## CONSOLIDATION

As soon as the vast extent of the New World began to unfold itself, steps were promptly taken to ensure its peaceable enjoyment, at anyrate as far as European intrusion was concerned. The Bull of Alexander VI. ought to have been sufficient to guarantee this in an intensely religious age, when the Holy See was regarded with superstitious reverence. But the occupants of the papal chair were mixed up too freely in political strife and ambition to gain much respect, and Charles V. himself was more than once in arms against the Pope, and once at least sacked Rome. How much he respected Papal Bulls may be judged by his action with regard to the Moluccas; and though he quibbled over, rather than openly broke it, he established a precedent for his enemies one day to follow, even had not the Reformation destroyed papal authority and made a merit of setting it at defiance.

We have already seen that Fonseca, afterwards Bishop of Burgos, was in pretty full control of colonial, or Indian affairs as they were called, when Columbus was preparing his second expedition. In 1501 the Casa de la Contratacion, or Board of Trade, was established at Seville, with Fonseca at its head, and had cognisance of every transaction that took place. It became a permanent institution, and exercised a greater inquisition than even a modern custom-house in a much protected country. Nothing could enter or leave Spain except under its supervision; and even when permission had been obtained to land imports, they were stored in the warehouses of the Board, and remained under its control until further permission was given to remove them; and this, particularly at such times as the treasury was ill supplied, was not an easy matter to arrange. But something more was wanted than merely to regulate trade, and in the year 1511 the Council of the Indies was established, which became the supreme authority of colonial government, as well as the final court of appeal, from the decisions of which there was no further redress. This council was reformed and finally perfected in 1542, when Charles V. enacted a code of regulations, which, with few alterations, remained in force until most of the colonies were for ever lost.

Such were the home arrangements, but after all the principal activity was in the colonies themselves. The immense rights conferred on Columbus and his descendants were sure to prove a bone of contention as soon as their value became more apparent. Fonseca was the first to attempt to undermine them, but he certainly had the goodwill of Ferdinand, who was no advocate of the rights of his subjects. Not only were the expeditions of Ojeda, Niño, and others, breaches of the agreement, but the appointment of Ovando as governor of Hispaniola was a direct violation of it, particularly when accompanied by a strict injunction to Columbus not to set foot on the island, against which he urgently protested. After his decease his son and heir, Diego, was equally persistent in asserting his claims; and it says a good deal for the administration of justice at that time, that in a suit brought by him against the Crown, the Council of the Indies gave a verdict in his favour. This was compromised by Diego Columbus relinquishing his claims to perpetual governorship in exchange for such grants and privileges as raised him and his family to a high position among the grandees of Spain, as well as conferred upon him a great fortune.

That left the way clear for such national arrangements as might be necessary. But it was only to be expected that future governors would look to the precedent of the Columbus agreement, and endeavour, whenever possible, to make similar provisions for themselves. This was certainly the object of Diego Velasquez, when he contemplated the conquest of Mexico, of the glory and profit of which Cortes robbed him. Pizarro was equally clamorous for the government of Peru, and undertook a special mission to Spain, to secure it for himself and Almagro who started on equal terms with him; but, as usually happens in such cases, he forgot all about his comrade-in-arms at the critical moment, and so prepared the way for that later dissension which rent the country in twain. Magellan acted upon exactly the same principle, and was assisted by Juan de Arandas, the head of the Board of Trade, who, by a special and private ageeement, was himself to profit in the venture to the extent of one-eighth, while one-fifth only of the total cargo brought home was to be reserved for the Crown; very different to Portuguese policy, which made eastern trade a government monopoly, and claimed everything, though it generally paid those who worked for it handsomely enough, and a residence of a few years in the colonies invariably meant a fortune. It was not, therefore, until all the original discoverers and conquerors were dead that it became possible to make effective and permanent regulations. The capital of Hispaniola was soon removed from Isabella on the north side of the island, to, in every way a more convenient and commodious harbour in the south, which received the name of San Domingo, and became the seat of government for the West Indies. The larger islands, like Porto Rico, Cuba, and Jamaica, were gradually colonised, but the smaller ones were left alone; it can well be understood that in the absence of any proved deposits of gold they were scarcely worth attention, and it was sufficient to keep a watch over them to defend them from the incursions of other nations. With the conquest of Mexico, however, the centre of gravity was moved farther west, and still more so when followed by that of Peru, because the only known route from the latter was by Panama and across the isthmus. Though Cortes lived until the last month of the year 1547 he was practically superseded in the government of Mexico some years earlier, as in 1540 Antonio de Mendoza, a scion of one of the greatest houses in Spain, was despatched as governor, with almost unlimited powers, and thus established the first of the two great viceroyalties into which the whole American continent was subsequently divided.

He was removed to Peru in 1550, and succeeded by Luis de Velasco, who retained the position fifteen years, and died at his post. Both were men of ability and integrity, and did their utmost for the interests of colony and Crown alike. Indeed, great wisdom was shown in the choice of most of the early viceroys, and in no case were they men who went out to exploit on their own account. It was not they who planted the seeds of decay, nor for that matter the government that appointed them ; and we must look for their dispersion to the vicious principles and habits of the colonists themselves, aggravated, it is true, by the false economic policy that was pursued, but which was then universally believed in, and not confined by any means to Spain.

Thus two great centres of authority were established in the cities of Mexico and Lima respectively. Perhaps the modern system which bears the closest analogy to it, may be seen in British India, where a viceroy exercises regal sway, and is upheld by a number of lesser dignitaries. The latter correspond to the eleven *audiencias*, or courts of judicature, appointed by Spain to settle all legal questions, in which the viceroys were not permitted to exercise any authority, the decisions being supervised by the Council of the Indies alone. The areas over which the eleven, to say nothing of the two governments, enjoyed control, were of course immense, and much delay as well as expense was entailed in settling disputes and obtaining justice ; but it is only fair to add that the *audiencias*, like the viceroyalties, were wonderfully free from corruption.

These areas, particularly the larger ones, were altogether too great for efficient oversight ; that of Mexico stretching from California in the north to Venezuela in the south, and including not only the West Indies, but the far removed Philippines, while that of Lima embraced the whole of South America both east and west of the Andes. The great territories included in the present Republics of Argentina, Uruguay, and Paraguay were looked upon as of little value, as they contained neither gold nor silver ; and as every attempt made to settle them only seemed to end in failure, little attention was given to their affairs. They became, indeed, a distinct source of loss to Spain, as they were found useful for purposes of contraband trade; and eventually the gold and silver, which could not be safely smuggled through the ordinary ports of shipment, were conveyed across the Andes and down the rivers to places of embarkation on the Amazon or Rio de la Plata, where foreign ships awaited the spoil and were ready to barter the coveted produce and manufactures of Europe in exchange. When these two viceroyalties were eventually subdivided, it was not into east and west, but north and south, and New Granada became the centre of one; while the territories now included in the United States were separated from Mexico, and constituted the other; but in neither case were the powers conferred on the new governors so great as the original.

Though the viceroys and *audiencias* were in the enjoyment of such extensive power and authority, they were restricted within well-defined limits. They were bound to act strictly upon enactments made in Spain, and had no legislative initiative of their own. True, they might put a very wide construction upon many of the laws laid down for their guidance, but even that was liable to be reversed by appeal to the Council of the Indies. Anything like self-government was entirely absent; one rigid cast-iron system bound the people of every clime and in every stage of progress alike, and it was most difficult to obtain any exemptions or concessions. We must not, however, be too ready to attribute such a policy to sheer stupidity, though there was undoubtedly much of that intense pride and stubbornness which is still characteristic of the modern

## CONSOLIDATION

Spaniard. Every other country in Europe would have acted much in the same manner, and as a matter of fact did so as soon as they got the chance.

Spain, of all countries, however, might at one time have been expected to work on broader principles. It was there civil and religious liberty first took root; but, alas, the tree which was so goodly to look upon, never bore much fruit. The persistent sapping by Charles v. robbed the people of most of their political privileges, and prepared the way for despotism pure and simple; while the religious bigotry of his immediate successors, Philip II. and Philip III., rarely equalled and perhaps never exceeded, destroyed every vestige of independence of thought. Not content with establishing the iniquitous Inquisition at home, it was everywhere imposed on the colonists, despite their emphatic protests, and the wonder is how even the native Indians escaped its clutches. There is always hope for a people oppressed by a secular tyrant; there is rarely any escape from ecclesiastical domination which has grown up with them, and attends them from the cradle to the grave. The latter was imposed at the most critical period in the history of America, nor has political independence yet secured more than a normal deliverance from the thraldom.

A system, so rigid that it refuses to bend, is bound in the long-run to break; and that is exactly what happened to Spain. Consolidation, or, as we call it nowadays, federation, is very well in its way, and may accomplish much that is beneficial to all concerned. But its first condition is elasticity, so that every section within its embrace may enjoy full freedom of expansion. There must be no jealousies, no recriminations, and, above everything, no attempts to get all and give nothing. These conditions are possible under an arrangement entered into freely by all parties; they are unattainable when imposed by the strong upon the weak. That is why Spain never won the gratitude of its colonies, why each and every one eagerly seized the opportunity of throwing off the yoke, and fought desperately for independence, and why, to-day, it is in its death-throes as a colonial power.

# VI

## RESTRICTION

IN its desire to retain exclusive possession of the New World, Spain could appeal to an important precedent. In the year 1479, when Ferdinand and Isabella had still to consolidate their kingdom by the final overthrow of the Moorish dominion in Granada, there was too much work at home to seek adventure abroad, and Portugal had little difficulty in obtaining a treaty by which its neighbour bound itself not to engage in African conquest. As far as the west coast was concerned, this was faithfully observed, though Ferdinand, in the later years of his life, and Cardinal Ximenes, as regent after his death, carried the war against the Moors to the African shores of the Mediterranean. By the Treaty of Tordesillas, Portugal, in its turn, bound itself not to encroach upon the possessions of Spain in the west, and it was the only power from which there was any imminent danger to be feared. But for all that, every possible precaution was adopted against the intrusion of foreigners; and as the discovery and conquest by Columbus had been made exclusively for the benefit of the Castilian Crown, even the Aragonese were included in this category; and, until the distinction between the two kingdoms was lost during the reign of Charles V., they were forbidden to take part in any of the numerous expeditions.

The Venetians and Genoese were the great shipowners and merchants of the age; and lest they, or any of the northern nations should be tempted to engage in the lucrative traffic, it was expressly enacted that no goods were to be shipped to or from America in any foreign bottom, unless a Spanish one was absolutely unavailable. Spaniards were prohibited from selling ships to foreigners, and a substantial bounty was offered to anyone who would engage in shipbuilding. Thus early was adopted that policy of restriction which was afterwards carried to such ridiculous extremes with such disastrous results.

It happened soon after the discovery of America, that the famous mercantile system and theories came into vogue among European nations. Under them there was a perpetual struggle to accumulate the precious metals, the possession of which was supposed to ensure wealth and well-being. It was but natural, therefore, that when Spain found itself mistress of the greatest supplies the world had ever known, it should guard them with jealous care, and use every means to prevent their dissemination. At all times the Crown claimed a large royalty on the mineral productions of the colonies, so large indeed, at first, as to be a practical monopoly. But from two-thirds, its pretensions were gradually lowered to one-half, one-third, and then to one-fifth, at which it remained constant. It can be well understood what a severe tax even twenty per cent. was upon mining industry, one that would to-day kill it in all but the very richest centres, though the cost of production is so immeasurably cheapened. It would have killed it then, had not the principal veins of ore proved to be almost pure metal, which required little more than extraction from the earth in which it

## RESTRICTION

was deposited. The royal fifth passing immediately into the hands of government officials in the colonies, appointed to collect it, would be safe in finding its way to Spain, but it was necessary to take every precaution that the remaining four-fifths went there too. This meant that there must be exclusive trade, and that everything the colonies wanted in exchange for their bullion must be obtained from the mother country.

To ensure that nothing should go astray, the channels of trade were narrowed as much as possible. Only one port in Spain was permitted to traffic with the Indies, Seville at first, and then Cadiz, as the ships employed increased in burden, and made river navigation somewhat risky. The whole manufacturing industry of the country became in consequence centred in that district, and so rapidly was it developed that, by the middle of the sixteenth century, there are said to have been 16,000 looms employing 130,000 people, engaged in Seville and its environs weaving woollen and silk fabrics, mostly for the American markets.

After the conquest of Mexico and Peru, the West Indian Islands sank into comparative insignificance, and attention was concentrated upon the mainland. There again the same system prevailed as at home. There were but two ports of arrival and departure—Vera Cruz for Mexico, and Porto Bello for the southern continent, though Carthagena eventually became a port of call. To reach Porto Bello everything from the west coast had to be first transported to Panama, and then across the isthmus. Once a year the galleons crossed the Atlantic, and on their arrival at Porto Bello the great fair was opened, and the entire business for twelve months had to be concluded within the forty days to which the fair was limited. Nor was any allowance made for possible expansion, the same number of ships departed each time with much the same cargo. It was all the better for the little coterie of Seville merchants who controlled the trade, if the shipments made did fall short of the demand, as then the fierce competition for the limited supply of luxuries, 'and even some of the necessaries, of the Old World, resulted in unusual quantities of bullion being offered in exchange for them. Silver the colonists could obtain in plenty again as soon as they got home; oil and wine, silks and linens, they must have now, or go without for a whole year. So that twelve months' produce of the mines, whether great or small, was frequently bartered for the merchandise borne by the galleons.

Everybody, from the king in his palace to the peasant in his hut, regarded the colonies simply as a source of revenue and profit to himself, and when they ceased to be this, they would be useless. The most stringent regulations were adopted, therefore, against trading, or even communicating amongst themselves, or of engaging in any industry, manufacturing or agricultural, which was not indigenous to the country; indeed, Spain insisted upon supplying everything it could grow or make which would stand the sea voyage, at its own price. The cultivation of neither the olive nor the vine was permitted in the New World, and severe penalties were inflicted upon anyone who had the temerity to disobey. Peru and Chili, however, were specially exempted, owing to their immense distance, and the damaged condition in which liquids generally arrived there, but they were not allowed to export the produce to any neighbouring country, and must consume it themselves. The duties of the colonists were, in fact, strictly limited to obtaining as much gold and silver as they could, while the Spaniards at home were to take care that they retained as little of it as possible. For all that, many fortunes were realised, principally by bullion being smuggled out of the country; and had there not been some such inducement, few men would have cared to expatriate themselves, and live amidst such uncomfortable surroundings.

The acme of folly was reached in the relationship which existed between the Philippines and the viceroyalty to which it was attached. With a stubbornness worthy of a better cause, Spain declined to hold any direct communication with the islands, long after Portuguese rights and claims in the East had become obsolete; it was not, indeed, until 1785 that any attempt was made to trade with its Eastern colony, and the last galleon from Acapulco to Manila only sailed in 1815.

The commerce between the two was for a long period limited to one galleon a year, despatched so as to arrive at Manila somewhere about the month of July. When foreigners began to prey on Spanish commerce, this galleon was carefully watched for, and not infrequently captured, so that as many as six consecutive seasons passed without the usual intercourse. It took with it regularly two million dollars in bullion, and half a million dollars' worth of consumable stores. The former was to pay for the goods purchased from the Chinese and other traders during the year, and these had always to be packed in fifteen hundred bales of exactly the same size. Whatever room was left in the vessel was allowed to be utilised by private shippers, whose principal excitement was speculating in the documents conferring this privilege upon their possessors.

The shipments of these merchants were never to exceed 250,000 dollars in value, nor were they allowed to take from Mexico more than 500,000 dollars in payment, a paternal government considering that one hundred per cent. was ample margin for freight, charges, and profit. As the articles most in demand in Mexico were silk and other manufactures of the Chinese, these were naturally given the preference, until a strong protest was lodged by the Seville merchants against the traffic, which, they maintained, competed with them; and an edict was actually passed in 1700 forbidding the shipment of anything from Manila to Acapulco save wax, spices, and other natural productions which could not be obtained from Spain. Even that did not soothe the ruffled temper of the Spaniard, who maintained that every dollar of bullion sent to the East, for whatever object, was taken out of his pocket.

Precisely similar principles were observed in all matters relating to government. Every office of profit under the Crown, almost every emolument, however trivial, was reserved for persons of pure Spanish birth. As a consequence, the official class was migratory, and remained in the colonies no longer than was necessary to accumulate a fortune or a competence, according to the taste of each individual member of it. Though there were honest and honourable men to be found among them, notably those filling the most exalted positions, that did not prevent the vast majority from preying on the colonists, many of whom, by virtue of the grants of territory they had received, attained to great influence and wealth. Their descendants were, nevertheless, debarred from all participation in either the legislative or executive functions of government, though they might have nothing but the purest Spanish blood flowing in their veins. Nor could they become dignitaries of the Church without much difficulty. In the days when the Holy See found it politic to be on good terms with the Spanish sovereign, the whole ecclesiastical patronage of the New World was vested in him and his successors; and though many Popes endeavoured to get this privilege back into their own hands, they always failed, and were compelled to confirm the nominations of the secular ruler. Both Mexico and Peru were rapidly overrun with clergy, secular as well as regular, and monastic establishments sprang up everywhere like mushrooms, yet preferment was always reserved for their brethren in Spain; and out of nearly four hundred bishops and archbishops consecrated up to the middle of the seventeenth century, scarce a dozen were taken from the Spanish-American community known as Creoles.

How this policy came to be modified,—abandoned it never was, and remains more or less in force in the remnant of the Spanish colonies to-day,—we shall have occasion to consider later on: necessity, that stern mother, gradually accomplished what would never have been yielded to any less persuasive influence.

After the unyielding conservatism of a century and a half, one concession rapidly followed another. In 1746 permission was granted to single ships to make the voyage to America, and to sail round Cape Horn, on condition that they were registered at, and traded only with the port of Cadiz in Europe. In 1764 a packet boat was despatched from Corunna once a month to

Havana and several other West Indian ports, while in the following year the trade was thrown open to the whole of Spain, with the result that that with Cuba tripled in ten years. In 1785 a Philippine Company was instituted to trade direct between Spain and the East, and all restrictions limiting its extent were removed. Holland, which had then attained to great importance in that part of the world, lodged a protest, on the ground that it was an infringement of the Papal Bull, which its own merchants had torn into shreds nearly two centuries earlier. Notwithstanding its great capital of 8,000,000 dollars, this company did not long prosper. In 1825 it was in a shaky condition, and appealed for an additional 4,500,000 dollars, to enable it to continue operations. In 1830 it entirely collapsed, and a few years later the trade with Manila was involuntarily thrown open to the world. The limit of 2,500,000 dollars, so long imposed, had expanded by 1841 to $3\frac{1}{4}$ million dollars of imports, and nearly $4\frac{1}{2}$ millions of exports; in 1885 the figures were 19 and $24\frac{1}{2}$ million dollars respectively; and in 1893 they had further risen to 25 and 30 millions. Similar results could be shown regarding Cuba; and though Spain still enjoys many privileges in both colonies, not extended to other countries, it has been able to retain only a very moderate percentage of this greatly increased commerce. What further extension it is capable of, if made absolutely free, and the territories and people of all colours and nationalities placed under wise and beneficent rule, is a question that time must be left to answer.

## VII

## OPPOSITION

FORTUNE favoured Columbus, in so far as the first natives of the New World with whom he came into contact were of a particularly mild and peaceable disposition. His policy might have been considerably modified, had he steered his ships the first voyage over the course he took the second, and met with the irreconcilable man-eating Caribs of the Lesser Antilles. Yet it did not often happen that either Columbus or his contemporary explorers encountered opposition on their first introduction to the different tribes, among most of which there was some family likeness. Means of communication between them there was little or none, only on rare occasions was the advent of strangers looked for, generally it was as unexpected as at San Salvador. It is proved, almost beyond possibility of doubt, that the two most civilised peoples of America, the Mexicans and Peruvians, were entirely ignorant of each other's existence. This fact was of material assistance to the Spaniards in their rapid subjugation of the continent, as they were able to take each separate part in detail, without so much as a dream of combination among them.

Had the wishes of the great navigator been respected, and the Indians treated with humanity and consideration, the conflict might have been long delayed.

Altogether avoided it hardly could have been, as long experience has proved that the coloured races of mankind can only be convinced of the superiority of the white man by force of arms, the sole argument to which they have ever been accustomed. The misbehaviour of the little colony left at Navidad in Hispaniola, however, at once opened the flood-gates and precipitated the deluge. There were chiefs and tribes in the interior of the island, very different to the gentle cacique Guacanagari and his dependants; but whether the Spaniards first baited the lion in his den, or the latter was on the prowl for prey, will never be known.

At anyrate, the second batch of colonists found their work cut out, and those who, like Alonso de Ojeda, loved fighting for fighting's sake, had no reason to complain. The first force of any magnitude they had to encounter consisted of ten thousand naked warriors, led by a cacique named Carnabo, and must have appeared formidable enough to the handful of men entrenched in the little fortress which was the object of attack. But the very fact that they were successful, not only raised the hopes, but afforded a new insight into the sort of warfare they would have to conduct. Whatever arms savages may possess, they always lack something of the accoutrements of the drilled battalion, and that something invariably wins the day against all odds. In this particular instance, it was not the firearms and cold steel, the former of which were contemptible enough and made more noise than havoc, but the horses and bloodhounds, the like of which had never been seen; for, strangely enough, the great West Continent was entirely devoid of large animals until they were introduced from Europe. The horses accomplished their work successfully, just in proportion as they had a dense solid mass to ride into and scatter right and left; the terrible ferocity of the dogs, as they tore man after man limb from limb, was absolutely irresistible. Thus, in most future encounters, these two branches of the service occupied a foremost place.

The contests in the islands were all much after the same pattern, and could never have had but one result; for, as the Spaniards increased in numbers, the natives were diminished by famine and fatigue, as well as by slaughter. The population of Hayti at the advent of Columbus was estimated to have been a million, yet, before many years had elapsed, the colonists were forcibly depopulating the smaller islands to provide a supply of labour sufficient for their limited requirements. It was the people of the mainland who might have been expected, and who actually did offer the stoutest resistance. No more wonderful campaign is recorded in military history than that conducted by Cortes against the Mexicans, and it may be doubted whether there was another man living who could have carried it to a successful issue.

Conspicuous as a general, he was unmatched as a diplomatist, whether in dealing with his own soldiers, his allies, or his enemies. Who else in that age would have dreamt, after defeating the Tlascalans against fearful odds, of enlisting them against their deadly foes the Aztecs, and so humouring them that they never swerved in their loyalty? Or who could have traded on the superstition of Montezuma, so as to gain complete control over his mind, and extract his treasures, valued at something like one and a half millions sterling, without a blow? But Montezuma once removed, the people who had long been accustomed to render him an unquestioned obedience, and to submit themselves to his slightest command, were free to follow leaders who evinced more spirit; and the death of that monarch was speedily followed by the *noche triste* with all its attendant horrors. To be captured alive, as many of the Spanish soldiers were, meant the most terrible of all ends, for they were hurried away to the temples, and their palpitating hearts torn from their living bodies, to be offered as a propitiation to the national deities. Yet even this did not disconcert Cortes and his brave adherents, who began immediately to concert another plan of campaign. The difficulties they had first encountered were as nothing compared to those they had still to face, for they had to deal with a victorious and determined foe, instead of a beaten and depressed one. Every obstacle, however, was overcome; and with the energetic assistance of allies, who little dreamt they were sealing their own doom and for ever sacrificing their independence, the powerful and rich kingdom of Mexico was finally brought into complete subjection to the Castilian Crown.

Of totally different and vastly inferior fibre was the conqueror of Peru. Pizarro was without either education or address—a rough, ambitious, and avaricious soldier. He, too, was favoured by internal dissensions, of which he could not possibly have known anything when he set forth on his errand. After a long period of peaceful and undisputed sway, the Inca dynasty was split by a feud between two brothers, one of whom, Atahualpa, had just asserted his superiority by force of arms, when the European conquerors appeared on the scene. A word from him, and not a man of them would have escaped alive. But at the critical moment an unaccountable paralysis overtook him, whether or not arising from a curiosity to see and interview the strangers, it is impossible to say. He realised his danger too late, for Pizarro, imitating Cortes, seized the person of the Inca, and the rest was rendered comparatively easy. Accustomed, like Montezuma, to exact unqualified obedience, he employed his subjects in collecting his ransom instead of fighting for his deliverance; and when the debt was almost paid, he found himself doomed to death instead of released from captivity. The forces of the empire were then scattered, and without a leader who could assume full authority. Still, many a desperate bid was subsequently made for freedom, but each time with less prospect of success, as the conquerors secured a firmer grip upon the country, until the execution of Tapac Amara, the last direct descendant of the Incas, in 1571, left a solitude which was called peace.

But after all it was not the opposition of the Indians, whether of the islands, of Mexico, or Peru, that proved the greatest danger to Spanish sovereignty. Enmity to Columbus, who was the accredited representative of the Crown and legal governor of the Indies, did not necessarily infer enmity to the Crown itself; indeed, those who rebelled against him were loud in their protestations of loyalty. Nevertheless, the turbulent factions fought for their own hand, and would have been equally opposed to any other governor who sought to place the necessary restraint upon their license. By permitting, and even compelling many of the discontented to return home, as well as by the temporary removal of Columbus himself, something like quiet was restored; but it is more than probable that had not the colonists been largely dependent upon Spain for many necessaries, not excluding food, they would have cut themselves adrift and refused to submit to the exactions upon their industry, or rather upon that of the natives from which they profited. More than once in the early days, the Home Government had to step cautiously, and commissions were despatched to ascertain where the grievances lay, and if possible redress them. They were mostly connected with labour; the majority of the clergy, to their credit be it said, ranging themselves on the side of humanity, and using all their influence to obtain ordinances favourable to the natives. As we have previously noticed, this difficulty was smoothed away to a great extent by the introduction of the African negro, which began as early as the year 1503.

The followers of Cortes were remarkably loyal to him in prosperity and adversity alike; and though for a long time he was unaware how his proceedings would be received at Court, he remained consistent in his devotion to his sovereign. His despatches breathe an almost effusive submission to their will and interests, and only his enemies ever laid any charges against him, while his own actions too obviously refuted them. It was only when some of his officers were removed from his influence and entrusted with commissions of their own, that they thought of kicking over the traces, and then it invariably happened that they were not in situations where any great harm could result. Mexico once subdued, long rendered the most willing obedience of any of the colonies, partly perhaps because under the direct influence of good and great viceroys, who acted both with intelligence and discretion.

It was far otherwise in Peru, where the duplicity of Pizarro in excluding Almagro from his proper share in the governorship roused the suspicion, then the ire, and finally the opposition of that honest and gallant soldier. When Pizarro returned from his visit to Spain, he was either accompanied or immediately followed by several of his brothers, who among them, formed a family compact for the protection and promotion of their own interests. To rid themselves of the rivalry of Almagro, they obtained for him the governorship of the country which now comprises the Republic of Chili. This, however, had still to be conquered, and the obstacles which presented themselves to the enterprise appeared so insurmountable, that Almagro and his followers abandoned it and returned to Cuzco, the rich capital of Peru, which the former maintained fell within the latitude of the patent granted to him. This assertion was naturally contested by the Pizarros, and in the civil war that followed, both Francisco Pizarro, the eldest and foremost of the brothers, and Almagro met with violent deaths. The Indians looked on with amazement at this strife between the white men, but failed to profit by it. Had they shown anything like the energy displayed in the warfare among themselves, or that of their Mexican brothers, they must inevitably have recaptured their kingdom, which it would have been extremely difficult to reconquer, but having allowed the golden opportunity to slip, it never again offered.

But the most serious menace to the supremacy of Spain in the New World occurred shortly after the promulgation of the edicts of Charles V. in 1542. The clauses guaranteeing the Indians their freedom, and protecting them against undue imposition, either of taxation or forced labour, were so obnoxious to the colonists, that something like a general rising was threatened. The tact of the Mexican viceroy pacified those under his rule, but Peru experienced the full force of an armed rebellion with all its evil consequences. The leader in this instance was Gonzales Pizarro, who had inherited the immense estates conferred upon the family by a grateful sovereign, and who now undoubtedly aimed at establishing a separate kingdom with himself its supreme head. Fortunately, the right man was again sent from Spain to deal effectively with this uprising, and though a cleric, Vaca de Castro exhibited the skill of a general and the diplomacy of a statesman. With the execution of Gonzales, the last of the Pizarro brothers, peace was restored; and by the middle of the sixteenth century the various governments were so effectively consolidated, that not for upwards of a hundred and fifty years did any revolt, Indian or Creole, meet with more than temporary success.

It was far otherwise with the Philippines, which have never been free for any length of time from disturbances of some kind. No effort indeed has ever been made to thoroughly subdue the turbulent natives; and there is no similar extent of territory under the control of a European government, about which so little is known regarding its natural resources and mineral wealth as the important islands of Luzon and Mindanao, which embrace half the total area of the archipelago. The principal ports have been strongly fortified, and reliance placed upon them to retain possession. The immunities enjoyed by the natives would, under ordinary circumstances, offer little inducement to revolt, but unfortunately the Philippines have from the very first been particularly subject to ecclesiastical influence and jurisdiction, and in its missionary and persecuting zeal the priesthood has made itself thoroughly obnoxious. The religious orders were the special object of animosity in the latest rising, and unless they are either suppressed, or placed under more effective political control, there will be little prospect of peace while Spain clings to the ownership of the islands.

In an epoch when most of the nations of Europe are struggling to add to their territories in the remotest corners of the earth, it seems almost incredible that four centuries ago a single one of them should have been permitted to annex a whole continent unchallenged. It was not so much the Pope's Bull that frightened competitors away, as the fact that they were too deeply absorbed in their own affairs. The importunity of Columbus had to wear itself nearly out before the fortunate completion of the Moorish conquest won it a more ready ear; and most other countries were about the same time either engaged in, or just recovering from, some similar internecine strife. Moreover, it was the energy of private adventurers rather than of the Spanish Crown which won for the latter a vast empire beyond the seas; nor was it until its value became plainly apparent that it was thought worth while to go to any great amount of trouble or expense in its development.

Similarly, the first external enemies the Spanish colonies had to encounter, were private and unattached adventurers. Piracy was an institution which had already flourished for many centuries. The Barbary corsairs were far more feared by the merchants of Venice and Genoa than the fiercest storms that ever visited the Mediterranean; and they had their counterpart in the Baltic, where the Hanseatic League carried on so extensive a commerce. It was only to be expected that they would sally forth from their inland seas when so much more valuable spoil was to be secured on the open ocean beyond, but strange to say, with the rapid decline of the trade which they had so long harried, their activity slackened, and their principles and profession were largely inherited by more civilised races. Some excuse was offered for this by the almost constant warfare that prevailed during the reign of Charles v., when France and Spain were at perpetual enmity, and England was found, first on one side, then on the other. The first important loss that befel Spain was the capture of the vessel conveying home the royal share of the treasures of Mexico by a French privateer, or pirate, as the Spaniards always preferred to call the ships which despoiled their fleets, a designation that was more often than not amply justified.

To begin with, these pirate ships were content to hang about the Azores, on the chance of meeting a caravel laden with treasure homeward bound. They gradually ventured farther west, until they actually arrived among the West Indian Islands, where they were surprised to find that altogether undreamt-of facilities awaited them for the pursuit of their nefarious trade. Though the entire Archipelago belonged nominally to Spain, only the larger islands were actually occupied, the smaller not being regarded as worthy of attention, until the Indian population of Hispaniola, Cuba, and Porto Rico, began to fail, and then they were raided for their inhabitants to supply the vacant places. With a scanty Spanish population, it would have been utterly impossible to fortify and inhabit all, even had colonists been found so self-denying as to banish themselves to places where the only chance of accumulating wealth was by hard work and steady application to agricultural pursuits.

For a long time these scattered islands were merely places of call, where fresh water and fruit could be obtained. No attempt was made at annexation in the name of any foreign power, and it would have been folly for any ship's company, even had they been disposed to relinquish their buccaneering career, to settle down and defy the Spanish power, whose forces would quickly have been put in motion to expel them.

Two events, designed by Philip II. to aggrandise the power of Spain at the expense of its neighbours, were eventually the means of arousing enmity against it to such an extent that the opposition of private adventurers was suddenly backed up by the full weight of the most rapidly progressing peoples and governments in the Old World.

Many previous efforts had been made to unite the Crowns of Spain and Portugal, but hitherto all had failed. The heroic death of Sebastian, however, in 1580, left the throne of Portugal without a direct heir, and among the numerous claimants was Philip, who overreached all his competitors. He was probably even then meditating that descent upon the liberties of England, which resulted eight years later in the despatch of the renowned Armada, and the writing of one of the most brilliant pages of English history. Success in the one instance, no less than failure in the other, created the most deadly foes that Spain ever had to encounter, until the persistent antagonism of Holland and England reduced it at last to a miserable shadow of its former self.

Philip's ruling passion was an intense bigotry, and from the moment he assumed sway in Spain and the

Low Countries, he sought to exterminate every trace of the Reformed faith. That brought him into conflict with the Dutch, whose principal port and city of Amsterdam was fast concentrating within itself the trade that Bruges and Antwerp had once commanded as the principal marts of the Hanseatic League. As Portugal extended its conquests in the East, Lisbon displaced Venice and Genoa, and became the great emporium of all Eastern produce, whence Amsterdam drew its supplies for distribution throughout Northern Europe. With the object, therefore, of destroying Dutch trade, Philip closed the port of Lisbon to it in 1594, fondly imagining that that would ruin his rebellious subjects, and enforce submission to his will.

He had entirely mistaken Dutch character, however, for in the following year the services were enlisted of Cornelius Hautmann, who had been a pilot in the Portuguese service; and he conducted the first Dutch expedition round the Cape of Good Hope on its way to open up a direct trade with the Spice Islands and India, which of course had become the property of Spain along with its own Philippines. Thus modestly was laid the foundation of the Dutch Empire in the East Indies, and when Portugal regained its freedom in 1640, under the House of Braganza, it found itself stripped of most of its former colonies, which were never to be restored.

Not content merely with retaining their former trade, the Dutch sought to extend it in other directions; and the incorporation of their East India Company in 1602 was followed by that of the West India Company in 1621, the operations of which were to embrace the west coast of Africa as well as the whole of Spanish America, in which the Brazils had then to be included. They had been preceded many years earlier by the English, who commenced operations in good earnest some time before the date of the Armada; indeed, those two great figures in English naval history, Sir John Hawkins and Sir Francis Drake, had then already performed their greatest exploits. As early as 1572, the latter gave a good account of himself on the Spanish Main, but his most daring feat was accomplished in 1578, when he sailed through the Straits of Magellan and appeared off the coast of Peru. Francisco Draques was the terror of Spanish America, and his was the name used to frighten Spanish American children when they were naughty.

A new danger thus became apparent, as the Spaniards had never dreamt before of reaching their West Coast possessions by the southern route. Lest other foreign adventurers should follow in the wake, an expedition under Pedro Sarmiento was despatched from Chili to explore the Straits and the adjoining territory, with the view, if practicable, of founding a strong colony and erecting substantial fortifications. Sarmiento's zeal outran his discretion, and after accomplishing his task he sailed for Spain, where he gave an exaggerated account, not only of the danger of leaving the Straits unprotected, but of the ease with which they could be rendered impregnable to all unfriendly visitors. A colony consisting of about four hundred souls was actually sent out in 1582, though from the very first it met with nothing but dire misfortune.

The captain-general commissioned to take charge of the undertaking, Diego Flores, disliked the job, and began by chartering the worst ships he could find. His lieutenant, Sarmiento, was more discreet in the choice of the embryo colonists, most of whom were skilled mechanics; but the fleet had scarcely left San Lucar on the outward voyage, when half of them were shipwrecked and drowned. Though replaced, disaster continued to follow upon disaster, the voyage being very much a repetition of the previous one made by Magellan, only in this instance the commander was himself the leading obstructionist. Eventually, rather more than two hundred souls sailed from the Rio de la Plata, and forty-five of these were drowned ere the Straits were reached. All but eight of the survivors subsequently perished, and the last of them was taken off in 1589 by the *Delight*, commanded by Sir John Cavendish, who appropriately named the spot where he found him "Port Famine."

The advent of the English and Dutch, followed half a century later by the French, led to the settlement of some of the unoccupied islands. They rapidly became something more than mere provisioning depôts, though several of them, and notably the island of Tortuga, were nothing else than the lairs of desperate crews of pirates, as reckless of their own lives as of those who were unfortunate enough to fall into their clutches. But Barbadoes and St. Christopher, St. Eustatius and Curaçao, Martinique and Guadaloupe, became the centre of something more legitimate, if quite as illegal, as sinking galleons and purloining their treasure, though that business was never missed either when the opportunity presented itself; and the Dutch West India Company alone is said to have been responsible for the capture of between five and six hundred Spanish vessels.

A great contraband trade sprang up, due almost

entirely to the severe restrictions imposed by the Home Government upon the colonists, who retaliated by seizing every chance that offered, not only of smuggling their treasure into Europe, but of exchanging it for those luxuries which their own manufacturers and traders dealt out to them with so parsimonious a hand. The galleons still continued to make their yearly voyages, but each time the profits became smaller, as the demand for the merchandise they carried was found to have been forestalled. This reacted upon Spanish industry at home, until not one-twentieth of the looms of Seville could afford employment to the native population. Even the regular trade that still remained passed into other hands, and though none but Spaniards were permitted to engage in it, it was done in Spanish names on foreign account. The commerce of the galleons, which at one time exceeded 15,000 tons each voyage, fell away until it hardly reached 2000, and represented little more than the royal fifth on such bullion as the owners felt bound to declare. Dutch and English manufacturers supplied the fabrics worn in America; and though the Spanish shippers through whom they were consigned might easily have refused payment on the ground that they were contraband, they retained their honour, even after they had little else to lose.

By degrees the Spanish Government was bound to recognise some of the privileges to which others had helped themselves. Under the Treaty of Utrecht, concluded in 1713, England was granted the privilege for thirty years of supplying America with 4800 negro slaves annually, and was also permitted to send a ship of 500 tons burden to the fair at Porto Bello. It was not long before the biggest 500-tonner that ever set sail regularly left an English port, and it was as regularly accompanied by a fleet of others. The South Sea Company, founded in 1711, knew a good deal about the contents of these vessels, or at anyrate their agents did; and, as fast as the merchandise was disposed of, it was surreptitiously replaced from the holds of the smaller ships, which were either cruising near at hand or anchored at some convenient port in the neighbourhood. Spain, in short, retained the territory and but little else. All that made it really valuable slowly but surely slipped through its grasp; the occasional capture of the galleons laden with treasure, in the days of Queen Elizabeth was but a trifling loss compared with the almost entire surrender of the commerce, which had taken place soon after the House of Hanover ascended the throne of England. Nor was it ever regained. The foreigner obtained so firm a foothold that nothing could shake him loose; and whether he carried on the traffic in his own name, or in that of someone else, he invariably managed to pocket the profits.

# VIII

## EXPULSION

IT rarely happened that an expedition was fitted out in a foreign port for the express purpose of capturing American territory. Trade and treasure were the objects desired, and when it was discovered that the Spanish colonists were ready enough to traffic with all comers, and pay handsomely for what they wanted, no idea was entertained of expelling them from their possessions. In the East, of course, it was different, because there the bulk of the trade was in the hands of the natives and of the Chinese, who came and went all the year round, and it was necessary to establish permanent depôts or factories in order to be always ready for them. The tactics pursued in the two hemispheres, therefore, were totally different, but the object was the same, namely to get into the closest possible relationship with those who controlled the local commerce.

Occasionally, some nation with which Spain was at war sought to deal it a blow in the West. Of the West India Islands, Hispaniola continued to be by far the most important, followed by Porto Rico and Cuba, with Jamaica a considerable distance in the rear, and the rest nowhere. By the middle of the seventeenth century, more than one European country was represented in some way or other, and as early as 1621 the

Dutch inaugurated the incorporation of their West India Company by the capture of the capital of Porto Rico, which however they did not long retain. The special aim of the company was the annexation of the Brazils, and they actually made some conquests there, and sent out a governor. But their most successful operations were conducted farther north, and Guiana became the real centre of Dutch power in the West, and the base from which Dutch traders carried on their illicit traffic with the Spanish possessions.

The English secured their first foothold in the neighbourhood by occupying the Bermudas in 1621, though this hardly brought them into direct contact with the West Indies. This was speedily followed by settlements in some of the unoccupied islands farther south. Barbadoes was taken possession of in 1625, and the same year St. Christopher, or St. Kitts as it is now called, was divided between the English and French. The former continued to add to their territory, taking Nevis in 1628, Antigua and Montserrat in 1632; and all these islands are so essentially English, as to prove conclusively that, although once nominally owned by Spain, Spanish influence was never exerted in them.

From 1650 until the period of his death, Oliver Cromwell, having established his authority at home, pursued an active foreign policy, and it was only natural that he should find himself in conflict with Spain, whose maxims of government, both civil and religious, were so utterly at variance with his. Thus, in 1654, a somewhat formidable fleet under the command of the admirals Penn and Venables, sailed for Barbadoes, where they would be ready for any emergency. Early the following year they made a descent upon Hispaniola, selecting the capital, San Domingo, as the object of attack. On the approach of the ships, the inhabitants, white and black alike, fled inland, but the affair was sadly mismanaged and somehow miscarried. Not wishing the expedition to prove a complete failure, the admirals set sail for the adjoining island of Jamaica, which did not then contain at the outside, more than 1500 whites, and perhaps as many blacks. This time, no difficulty was experienced, and the island was taken formal possession of, this being the first loss of occupied territory inflicted upon Spain, as well as the most important acquisition ever made in the West Indies by England. In 1658 the Spaniards attempted to drive the intruders out but failed, and in 1670 a treaty was entered into between the two countries, in which Spain recognised the rights of England both in Jamaica and the smaller islands of which possession had been previously taken.

About this time also, the French West India Company was incorporated, the brilliant finance minister of Louis XIV., Colbert, not liking to be without a hand in the game. He began in a more legitimate fashion than his competitors, and in 1664 purchased the rights of the settlers in Martinique, Guadaloupe, St. Lucia, Grenada, and a few other islands for about a million livres. Spanish tyranny, however, afforded an excuse for more high-handed proceedings, and the company secured a footing on the western side of Hispaniola, Spanish interests being concentrated almost entirely on the eastern. The settlements so established became little more than a rallying-point and shelter for buccaneers, who, in consequence of their roving habits, were difficult to eject, until eventually this intermittent occupation of a portion of the island induced France to lay claim to the whole, but the cession was only formally recognised by Spain more than a century later. Thus the four predominant powers of Europe all had a stake in the Western Hemisphere.

Nearly a hundred and fifty years elapsed without witnessing any further important changes. The very vastness of the Spanish American Empire was its principal protection. Europe was growing thoroughly accustomed to immense armies, but they could only be moved on land, and there was no means for transporting them across the sea. What chance was there then of conquering a territory which extended uninterruptedly from California to Chili, and from Florida to the Rio de la Plata, even had there been much inclination? The idea, it is true, occurred more than once, and especially in 1702, when, the death of Charles II. of Spain having brought to an end the Hapsburg dynasty, and the Wars of the Spanish Succession were entered upon, an alliance was formed between England, Holland, and the German Empire for the conquest of the Spanish colonies, but like others it came to nothing. Again, in 1739, Spain, alarmed at the growing contraband trade, insisted very justifiably in searching English ships in American waters, but this was resented and led to war, in which Porto Bello was captured, and that had something to do with the permission granted a few years later to trade by the longer, but safer and more convenient route round Cape Horn.

Once more, in 1762, what was known as the Family Compact involved the rest of Europe in hostilities against the Bourbon dynasties in France, Spain, and Italy, and the war was carried both to the East and

West Indies. Havana and Manila were captured by the English, and might have become English possessions, had not the Treaty of Paris, concluded in 1763, brought the campaign to an end, and made it a condition that all colonial conquests were to be restored to their original owners. Minor changes were frequent and numerous, but they were generally a mere shuffling of the cards between England, Holland, and France, leaving the Spanish possessions much as they were.

The eighteenth century, as it drew to its close, found the Spanish occupation of America, almost as it had been in the first half of the seventeenth. Then a mighty upheaval was witnessed both in North America and Europe, and the War of Independence in the United States, together with the French Revolution, provide the sequel for what followed in South America. Scarcely a murmur was heard in the principal Spanish colonies while these great events were changing the destinies of the civilised world, and an onlooker who had time to think must have been astonished at their apparent loyalty to the mother country, oppressed though they had been, and still were, while everywhere else the blow for freedom was being struck. Perhaps another conclusion might have been arrived at, namely, that the ancient Spanish stock had so degenerated, and had become such a mean-spirited race, that it dare not act like its neighbours farther north; but subsequent events disproved this hypothesis. The Girondists and the Mountain rose and fell; Napoleon became successively director, dictator, emperor—still no sign of movement. Then the moment arrived for the arch-disturber of Europe to overthrow the ancient monarchy of Spain, and to establish a brand new one with his brother

Joseph at its head. That was the supreme crisis to make a move, or for ever to remain still. Spain almost to a man resented the affront. Spanish America joined the mother country, and refused to recognise the upstart dynasty.

Still, in the midst of this death-like calm, some presages of the coming storm were discernible. In the first place, France, by the Treaty of Basle in 1795, secured the cession of the whole of Hispaniola, only, however, in a few years to lose it again by its declaration of independence, and the formation of a black republic. In the naval conflicts so frequent during that disturbed period England both lost and gained. The Dutch and Spanish were both unwilling confederates of Napoleon, but their connection with him, nevertheless exposed their foreign possessions to the attack of his declared enemies; and England captured Demerara and Essequibo in Guiana from the former, and the island of Trinidad from the latter. All these were trivial acquisitions, compared with the vast extent of Mexico and Central America, Peru, and New Granada, and the eastern province of Buenos Ayres. Brazil had reverted to Portugal with the firm establishment of the Braganza dynasty, and was nearly all there was left of its once great colonial empire. In March 1808 the ill fortune of the royal family drove them from their own kingdom to find refuge beyond the seas, and Brazil became an independent empire under the fugitive Portuguese sovereign, whose descendants remained in peaceable and prosperous possession until the revolution which dethroned the late ill-fated Dom Pedro.

These changes were due entirely to foreign intervention and not to domestic unrest. The first sign of this was when Francisco Miranda, a Spanish American who had fought under Washington, conceived the idea of freeing his fellow-countrymen, and took steps with that object by founding a " Gran Reunion Americana " in London in 1806. But so unresponsive were the inhabitants of the Spanish Main, that the first active movement of the league resulted in dead failure. It attracted the sympathy and support, however, of two active and capable men, Bolivar and San Martin, who were destined to do so much for the emancipation of South America from European bondage, and whose advent brought a rapid change in the feeling of indifference with which the movement was regarded.

Still, the loyalty of the colonists might have been proof against their blandishments had the Government of Ferdinand VII., established at Cadiz in opposition to that of Joseph Buonaparte, shown itself in any way conciliatory towards them. Loyal though the Spaniards at home were to the Bourbon dynasty, they were only willing to rally round it, on condition of the carrying out of many important reforms in consonance with the spirit of the age ; and the colonists likewise demanded that, as the price of their adhesion, they should be put upon an equality with Spain, and be accorded perfect liberty in their agricultural and manufacturing industries; that trade should be thrown open between all the countries on the American Continent and with the Philippines ; and that all restrictions and monopolies should be abolished, and fixed duties substituted in their place. Reasonable though these demands now appear, they were indignantly rejected, and with one consent nearly every country in Spanish America was ablaze with revolution.

One of the earliest outbreaks was in Mexico, the near

proximity of the United States having perhaps inspired in that country a more intense longing for freedom than elsewhere. A small band of patriots had for some time been watching an opportunity for asserting themselves, and with Hidalgo and Allende at their head, took the extreme step of issuing a declaration of independence on the 16th September 1810. Spanish influence was still strong, and in less than a year the outbreak was suppressed, and the leaders executed. Others rose to take their places, and just three years after the declaration of independence, the first Mexican Congress was summoned to meet at the town of Chilpantzongo, which was in the hands of the insurgents. Morelos, the principal actor at this stage of the drama, was captured and shot in December 1815; but that only imposed a temporary check on the movement. In the delusive hope of regaining full control, Ferdinand, then firmly re-established on his throne, offered concessions in 1820, but it was too late, and they failed to effect a pacification. Independence was once more declared in 1821, but this time at the instigation of a dictator who aimed at founding an empire for himself, and who did for a short period sway the destinies of his country as the Emperor Iturbide I. His reign was brief, and a republic was definitely established on the 16th December 1823, the subsequent career of which has been so chequered until quite recent times. Having been recognised by the principal Courts of Europe, Spain itself accredited an ambassador in 1839, and made no further efforts to reassert its former title.

Elsewhere the struggle was less prolonged, though, while it lasted, quite as exciting. At the instigation of Bolivar, Venezuela proclaimed its independence in July

## EXPULSION

1811, and several years later united with New Granada as the Republic of Colombia. Buenos Ayres established a junta in 1810, a constituent assembly was called in January 1813, and entire independence of Spain was declared, July 1816. The insurrection in Chili likewise began in 1810, when a national congress was summoned to meet at Santiago; but the Spanish interest was strong on the west coast, and it was not until San Martin crossed the Andes from La Plata in 1817 that independence was made good. Material assistance was afforded by the famous Admiral Cochrane (Lord Dundonald), who, driven in disgrace from his native country, placed his services at the disposal of the revolting Chilians, and gave them that naval pre-eminence in South America, which they have ever since retained.

Peru proved an even tougher job, but the combined forces of San Martin and Cochrane proved irresistible, and both Lima and Callao were taken in 1821. Lima, however, was recaptured by the Spaniards in 1823, but Bolivar, marching against it from Colombia, was appointed dictator, and gained so decisive a victory in 1824, that the Spanish army was forced to capitulate, and by 1826 the connection with the mother country was completely and finally severed. Spain had vainly striven against these successive misfortunes, and in 1815 sent out a considerable force under Marshal Morillo, who gained a few temporary successes, but his cruelties and atrocious conduct only exasperated the colonists, and instigated them to greater exertions. The various countries of Central America were quietly federated into the Republic of Guatemala in 1823, in the absence of any Spanish troops to oppose; and thus, from the northern borders of Mexico to the southern confines of Chili and La Plata, the conquerors of the New World were for ever ejected. England was the first to recognise the South American Republics, and entered into commercial treaties with several of them in 1825, after which date Spain can no longer be said to have been able to claim ownership of a single acre on the American Continent.

# IX

## RETENTION

WHILE the events recorded in the previous chapter were taking place on the Spanish Main, a strange quiescence pervaded those islands of the West Indies which still acknowledged the Spanish dominion. Mexico, Peru, Chili, Buenos Ayres, slipped through the feeble grasp of their nominal owners one after the other; Cuba, the Pearl of the Antilles, as its inhabitants love to call it, and Porto Rico, still remained out of the wreck of a once vast colonial empire. What were the forces at work which there prevented the assertion of independence made good elsewhere?

To begin with, the economic conditions were totally different. Negro slavery was the predominant feature in the islands; it never made much headway on the mainland of the Southern Continent outside Brazil, for reasons already stated. Constitutional independence is the bitterest foe of human bondage, and though both existed side by side in the United States for more than half a century, the day arrived when one or other had to succumb; and everyone now rejoices to think that the cause of freedom came off triumphant. The wealth of the Spanish American colonist lay principally in his boundless territories and what they were capable of producing; and the former, at anyrate, if subject to alienation, were at least impossible of removal. The

Cuban planter reckoned as his most precious possession the flesh and blood attached to his estates, and the very words "freedom" and "independence" stank in his nostrils. Whatever inconvenience, therefore, he suffered from his political connection with an effete monarchy and a decaying or decayed empire, he at least felt that, while he clung to it, it would afford him protection for his property.

A steady flood of immigration from the mother country has maintained this connection down to the present day. The wealthiest merchants and planters have invariably been of pure Spanish blood, and their contempt for the Cuban creoles, though many of them are as pure-blooded as themselves, and have no taint whatever of the "tar-brush," has helped to maintain them as a separate class, regarded as intruders by all of Cuban birth, and hated accordingly. They have of necessity invoked Spanish aid and relied on Spanish authority, and have, for nearly a hundred years, provided the basis for Spanish rule in the island. Many of them made their fortunes and returned home, leaving room for others to follow. Some have made Cuba their permanent domicile, but invariably with fatal effects upon their offspring, for Cuban birth is almost synonymous with Cuban sympathies, and in any rising, the father who has been on the side of the Crown, has witnessed his sons throwing in their lot with the rebels.

Ever since the emancipation of the Spanish Main, Cuba has been in a state of political unrest. Various secret societies have been constituted, and have received advice and assistance from Mexicans, Chilians, and others who had already succeeded in throwing off their own fetters. In 1823 the Society of Soles struck a blow for liberty; six years later it was the Company of the Black Eagle which attempted success where its predecessor had failed. Both were essentially Creole risings, and although those who participated in them freely gave expression to their abhorrence of slavery, no assistance was either asked or received from the negroes. For these unfortunates, however, failure meant the tightening of their bonds; and it is not surprising to find that in 1844, goaded to despair by their sufferings, they tried an insurrection on their own account, though of course it ended disastrously.

These outbreaks were all more or less localised, and it was not until 1868 that a revolution broke out, destined to involve the entire island, and to occupy long and weary years in suppressing, if, indeed, the smoking embers can be said ever to have been quenched. It was undoubtedly instigated by the American Civil War, which had ended in the uncompromising abolition of slavery, and so raised the hopes of the friends of liberty in Cuba. Though the planters and slave-owners ranged themselves, as was natural, on the side of law and order, their enthusiasm was no longer of the keenest. They realised that the institution to which they clung so tenaciously was doomed, and it became a question with them of doing the best they could for themselves. Emancipation in the British West Indies had for a time added enormously to their prosperity, until the value of slaves underwent so great an appreciation, that it no longer became profitable to purchase them, and only actual owners derived any benefit. For it must be remembered there was a distinct difference between the slave trade and slavery, and long after public opinion revolted against, and prohibited the kidnapping and traffic in human flesh, it continued to tolerate its ownership, and recognised natural increase as legitimate property. That African negroes were smuggled into Cuba is tolerably certain; nevertheless, the numbers were too small to prevent the gradual increase in value of an able-bodied male slave from £50 to something like £350 or £400. This was the surest means of eventual abolition; for while this high price set upon the black made him valuable property, and ensured his better treatment, it tended to make the luxury too costly, and one that could eventually no longer be indulged in, as the point must be reached where free labour would become cheaper.

About the time of the rebellion, the number of slaves in Cuba was between 350,000 and 400,000, and their value on paper was simply enormous. The £20,000,000 voted by the British Parliament as compensation to the disinherited slave-owners in the British West Indies, would have been but a drop in the ocean in any scheme for Cuban emancipation by purchase. Indeed, to do the planters justice, they never expected anything of the sort, and all the more practical of them asked, was to be let down gently. This was effected by the proclamation of what was known as the Moret Law in 1870, which at once declared free all slaves over sixty years of age, and decreed that every child born after that year should be free likewise. In the first instance, the planters registered a distinct gain, as they got rid of a number of old and decrepit dependants no longer fit for work; but this was offset by the compulsory maintenance, until their eighteenth year, of all the free offspring of their slaves. Under this law, the odious institution perished in something like twenty years, because its burdens gradually outweighed its benefits, until the low wage for which the free negro is willing to work, became the more economical method of production.

Thus the strongest tie between Spain and Cuba was snapped, and the party of independence gained force, as many planters found no longer any advantage in supporting the authority of the Crown. The rebellion dragged on; the Spanish troops continually poured in having to encounter the guerilla warfare, with which we have become so well acquainted during the present revolution, and for which the division of the island affords so many opportunities. For, considerable though the population is, two-thirds of it has always been concentrated in the western corner, of which Havana is the capital, the remaining districts being very sparsely peopled. It is in these rebellion has always thriven; and the policy adopted by General Weyler, when in supreme command, was to make them a desert by destroying all sustenance, and forcibly removing the inhabitants, who, under the name of Reconcentrados, have since roused so much sympathy, not only in the United States, but in other countries as well, owing to the terrible deprivation and suffering they have had to undergo.

Though the outbreak of 1868 was eventually suppressed, it left a legacy of bitter memories and still bitterer exactions. For, true to its policy of four centuries, Spain determined that it at least would not be a loser, and saddled the entire cost of the military operations, and nobody knows what else besides, on the unfortunate island, in the form of a debt amounting to about eighty millions sterling. Even this might have been tolerated had any attempt been made to establish an equitable system of government, because an era of prosperity set in which culminated in 1891, when the total exports were valued at no less than £20,000,000, and there was ample margin for interest on an inflated debt. But the rapacity of Catalan manufacturers, no less than of government officials, upset everything; and from the captain-general down to the humblest trader in Barcelona, all expected to pocket something out of the spoils of Cuba. Nor is the plunder limited to Spaniards. Despite the restrictions against trading by foreigners, adventurers of all nationalities manage to get a foothold in Havana, and corruption preys on corruption. No one in fact is expected to be honest, and a stranger remarking upon the rascality prevailing in high places, would as likely as not be met with a shrug of the shoulders and the reply, *Robamos todos*, "We are all thieves." Excessive import duties answer the purpose of nearly every merchant and petty trader, because they enable them to exact high prices from customers on goods which have been smuggled and never paid any duties at all, beyond a certain amount of blackmail to the customs officials. Some of the imports must of course pay the full tariff, if only as a blind, but how much of the actual receipts eventually find their way to the exchequer is quite another matter.

While fortunes are being thus accumulated, somebody must provide them; and as a matter of fact they are wrung out of the unfortunate population of the island, which a few years ago numbered nearly 1¾ millions, of whom but a few are among the privileged or robber class. That the majority should rise against such exactions, backed as they are by political oppression of the very worst type, is not to be wondered at—the marvel indeed would be were there no rebellion. The privilege of returning sixteen senators and thirty deputies to the Spanish Cortes is at best an empty one, inasmuch as that body exercises very little authority at home, and none at all abroad. What is wanted is fair and honest government in the island itself, whether under the nominal control of another power or not. That American interference is resented is not unnatural, that this interference is not always disinterested is certain. But beneath all the scheming of trusts and capitalists, and the love of adventure of mere filibusters, there is deep down in the minds and hearts of the American people an utter repugnance for the political system of which Cuba affords an illustration. Whatever may have been the case in the past, it is now impossible for any right-minded man to be free without wishing the same freedom for others, always with the reservation that they know how to use it aright. Cuba may not yet be ripe for a British or an American constitution, but Englishmen cannot fail to sympathise with the outburst of humanitarian and political feeling in the United States, which dwarfs every meaner and unworthier motive.

# X

## SUCCESSION

It is no part of my task to follow the history of the Spanish American States after the severance of the connection with the European country which gave them birth. London financiers, and British investors generally, would probably be the best people to go to for a detailed history of the actions of the South American Republics during the last fifty years, which, so far as the majority of them is concerned, may be summed up in the two words, revolution and repudiation.

Long before its expulsion, however, Spain had ceased to exercise a predominating influence on the American Continent. Another power had risen in the north; the people who contributed to its ever-growing strength were not enervated by the prospect of untold wealth, gathered by the labour of others, but rather were compelled to wring a meagre subsistence out of the earth by the sweat of their brow. By long usage, succeeding generations of Spanish Americans had become accustomed to the severe restrictions and unnatural discipline imposed upon them, and grew listless, only seeking redress by oppressing in turn the unfortunate Indians and negroes subject to them. For all this lethargy they have since made ample amends; but it would have been better for themselves, and infinitely better for their descendants, had they earlier put forth their energies, and won more gradually the liberties, which when attained were so signally abused. Without a tithe of the incentive, the Anglo-Saxon American first resented, and then successfully resisted interference with his liberties and his progress; and, by the blow which he struck for both, attained that manly self-reliance and independence, which has made him the foremost figure on the continent he inhabits, if not in the whole world.

What were, at the beginning of the present century, the two great powers in America, Spain and the United States, were brought into close contact through the possessions of the former on the northern shores of the Gulf of Mexico. Louisiana had been subjected to a series of deals between France and Spain, until, while in possession of the former, Napoleon saw an opportunity of converting a then somewhat useless dependency into that ready cash, which was so necessary for the promotion of his European ambitions. James Monroe, who subsequently became the author of the now famous doctrine which bears his name, was despatched by his Government, as ambassador-extraordinary, and negotiated the transfer of the State for sixty millions of francs, much more than was then regarded as its value, but not too high a price to pay when the increase of territorial importance which it gave the purchaser is taken into account.

Spain still retained Florida, a name at one time given to territory extending as far north as Virginia, and westward to the Mississippi Valley, but then confined to little more than the area at present included in the State. By further negotiation, this was likewise acquired, and the United States became master and sole proprietor of the entire territory from the great Lakes to the Gulf. Spain having been finally expelled, no further acquisitions were possible at its expense. Mexico, when wrenched from its grasp, still included the rich territories of Texas, New Mexico, and California ; and the United States, having reached its utmost limits in one direction, soon sought for extensions in another. Northwest there was no other opponent to be faced than the rapidly disappearing Red Indian ; south-west, though Spain had gone, Spanish pride and tenacity remained. Under the guise of colonisation, the Mexican boundaries were gradually encroached upon, until the Rio Grande was tacitly recognised as the separating line. Partly by purchase, and partly by warfare, not it is to be feared always very justly waged by the United States, Texas gradually assumed its present dimensions, which render it well worthy of the designation of the Empire State. California and New Mexico, together with part of Texas, were acquired in 1848 for fifteen million dollars ; and almost immediately after, the great rush for gold occurred, the discovery of which, in almost simultaneous conjunction with the rich find in Australia, proved such a disturbing element in the economic conditions of the civilised world. Thus the United States became the greatest single inheritor of the vast estate which had once belonged to Spain.

Though not eager for further extension, the Republic was determined that no other power should obtain territory in the New World. This was expressed in the message sent by President Monroe to Congress in the year 1823, in which referring to the European powers, he said : "We should consider any attempt on their part, to extend their system to any portion of this hemisphere, as dangerous to our peace and safety"; and this constitutes the basis of the Monroe doctrine. A suspected intention on the part of Spain to reconquer its rebellious colonies, backed by what was known as the Holy Alliance, was the circumstance that gave rise to this important declaration, which has since been either applied or threatened, indiscriminately to every other European power.

France was the first to be reminded of its existence, and to experience its efficacy, after it had lain dormant for more than forty years. For reasons best known to himself, Napoleon the Third, during the American Civil War, imposed a scion of the House of Austria upon the Mexican Republic, and promised Maximilian, when elected Emperor, ample assistance to consolidate his power. The United States, however, were not so absorbed in their own affairs, as not to know what was taking place among their neighbours; and a resolution passed by the House of Representatives on the 4th April 1864, against the establishment of the monarchical government in Mexico, convinced Napoleon that he had made a mistake. Had the Mexicans themselves proved willing, such interference would have been altogether unjustifiable, but unfortunately for Maximilian, the national feeling against him was intensely strong, and he refused to take the warning acted upon by his more astute instigator, with fatal consequences to himself, and ruin to his family.

The Venezuelan dispute with Great Britain is but another phase of the same policy, which has undergone a rapid development during the last few years, so rapid indeed that the world is beginning to wonder where it will eventually lead to. A Papal Bull may have been effective to award an entire hemisphere to a single country in the fifteenth century; no such bull or edict, issued by the strongest power that ever existed, would stand any chance of acceptance to-day.

The question agitating people's minds at present, however, is to whom the succession of the remaining Spanish colonies is eventually to revert. It is becoming more and more improbable that Spain will be able to retain them; the display of impotency in suppressing the insurrections both in Cuba and the Philippines proving not only that its government of these islands is obnoxious to their inhabitants, but that its methods are out of harmony with modern sentiment. It is too late in the day to subject the interests of any intelligent and moderately progressive community to the necessities and requirements of another people thousands of miles away; and the financial position of Spain is now so desperate, that unless it can continue to derive a large net revenue from its foreign possessions, it must face insolvency. It has been a matter of surprise how the immense sums necessary to continue the conflict were raised; and the only solution is to be found in the support accorded by foreign creditors, who were too deeply involved to permit a collapse. While some sort of a hold, no matter how feeble, could be kept on the colonies, they were a more or less valuable asset; but had the insurgents once succeeded in driving out the Spanish troops, and asserted their independence, they were hardly likely to allow themselves to be burdened with the debts and responsibilities of a defeated foe. The £80,000,000 already hanging round the neck of Cuba, mostly expended to bind the island to an effete and reactionary power, handicaps its industries to a frightful extent; and it is difficult to see how for some years to come, after the great destruction of property that has taken, and may yet take place, it is to meet the ordinary expenses of internal government, much less interest on so large a debt, materially increased were the Spanish connection to continue on its present basis.

Prior to the actual outbreak of hostilities between the United States and Spain, several possible solutions of the problem offered. Had Spain been willing to sacrifice its pride in the interests of its pocket, or rather of its creditors, an easy way might have been found out of the difficulty. If left to open competition, there would, a year or two ago, have been eager purchasers of the island, had it not been for the risk of political complications. Cuba could be rendered enormously productive by energetic capitalists who felt their tenure secure; and before the German Kaiser found an outlet for his ambitious projects at Kiaou Chow, he would probably not have grudged the loss of a few years' interest on the £50,000,000 or even £100,000,000 outlay, necessary to acquire so promising a possession as Cuba. But he would hardly have risked another fifty or hundred millions on a war with the United States, in which at the best only a temporary victory could have been secured.

Acquisition by the United States was another possibility, could terms have been agreed upon. But here the conflicting interests within the United States themselves were far more intense than between that Republic and Spain. Capitalists, representing concerns like the Sugar and Tobacco Trusts, would have been enthusiastically in favour of such a course at the national expense, because they would, for a time at anyrate, have profited enormously by the deal. The political future, however, is much too uncertain to permit them to risk their own money, and public sentiment is entirely opposed to the admission of a numerically important alien race to the privileges and responsibilities of the Union. The alternative of annexation without representation, would not be tamely submitted to by the Cubans, who yearn for nothing so much as an opportunity to display their talents for self-government.

Independence, guaranteed by the United States, appears at present the most feasible, but the situation is so kaleidoscopic that a change may take place at any moment, for it looked at one time as though blood might assert its pre-eminence, and Cuban combine with Spaniard to resist the intrusion of the foreigner. That indeed would have been a strange climax, but one that it appears we are not to witness, as friendly relations have been established between insurgents and United States officers. It can only be hoped that this will assist in bringing about, at no distant date, such a settlement as will be welcomed by the entire civilised world.

The Philippines are to a great extent an unknown quantity, and their productiveness is at best a matter of conjecture. There is a far better prospect, however, of concluding a deal with them. But again political complications may ensue. It goes without saying that no European power could acquire them without rousing the jealousy of its neighbours, particularly after recent events in China, though it might not actually lead to hostilities. But Japan is undoubtedly casting covetous glances that way, and would not willingly permit another power to step in. It has already taken possession of the half-way house, the island of Formosa, and is as anxious to further extend its territories as any State in the West. The intervention of Russia has barred it for the present, and probably for all time against expansion on the Asiatic Continent, as Russia ever advances, never recedes. There is still scope, however, for the most aggressive ambition in the Archipelago of the Eastern Seas ; and should Japan secure it, with its lucrative trade, and possible mineral wealth, Russia on the Yellow Sea would be in close contact with a neighbour by no means to be despised. The naval activity of the Japanese Government has been attributed to a desire to pay off old scores against its hitherto too powerful opponent ; it may easily forget the desire for revenge in the opportunities offered elsewhere for aggrandisement.

The final collapse of Spain as a colonial power is likely therefore to be attended with some political problems of the first magnitude. When South America revolted and secured its freedom, the European nations were too exhausted to dream of grabbing at the spoil. Now everything is different. Bloated armaments cry aloud for some excuse for maintenance ; the commercial spirit of the age demands new markets for its enterprise ; and the lust of territory is no longer confined to the rounding off a border, or the addition of a trumpery State, but requires for its insatiable maw square miles by the million. A stronger power than Spain would have found it hard to resist such pressure. Nor is the difficulty overcome by the capture of Manila and the virtual control of the islands by the United States fleet. It is too soon yet to decide whether the Republic will make an effort to remain in permanent possession. Should it do so, and thus involve itself in the turmoil of what has become European politics, a new factor will have been introduced into them, the force of which it is utterly impossible to calculate.

# PRESS OPINIONS

ON

# "TARIFF AND TRADE."

———

*Spectator.*—"Experience has taught us some distrust of a writer on an economical subject who begins by appealing to business experience as against professional theory. We hasten to add that any misgivings we may have conceived on this account from Mr. Root's preface have been effectually dissipated by a further study of his book. We have, in fact, seldom come across a more satisfactory popular statement of the arguments in favour of the well-tried fiscal and commercial policy of this country than is presented in the twelve chapters in which Mr. Root analyses the tariffs of the principal commercial states, and traces their effects on the well-being of the people."

*British Trade Journal.*—"By far the ablest of the numerous works recently published on the tariff question is that under the above title by Mr. J. W. Root. He writes throughout, not as a doctrinaire, nor even an amateur political economist, but as a practical business man, who can discuss the subject without the drawback of preconceived theories. The scope of the work is very wide, embracing as it does all the questions arising from a nation's fiscal policy."

*Commerce.*—"One very excellent feature about this book is to be sincerely commended—it is quite free from fanaticism. . . . An exceedingly useful and thoughtful book."

*British Australasian.*—"Mr. Root's treatise is a useful work to colonists in these days of discussions upon imperial *Zollvereins* and suggested forms of federation of the British Empire. . . . Though a long and exhaustive work, *Tariff and Trade* is quite up to date as to the subjects and theories handled."

*Antigua (W. I.) Standard.*—"The free trade and the protective policies, of which we hear so much in connection with our own industries, are fully explained in an attractive style, so that he who runs may read and be delighted in the reading; and although written in defence of the former, even the most prejudiced reader will find much in *Tariff and Trade* to instruct him."

# PRESS OPINIONS

*Liverpool Daily Post.*—"When a business man takes to the study of economics, and has sufficient power of detachment to rise above the narrow sphere in which his own interests lie, and to use his special knowledge as a constant check upon theoretical ideas, he has a great advantage over all other people. This is the position Mr. J. W. Root occupies in discussing *Tariff and Trade*. Mr. Root has a rare faculty for acquiring statistical and other information as to the trade and taxation of various countries, of subjecting his facts to analytical examination, and of placing his conclusions before the public in the light of the accepted economic theories of the day. . . . Throughout the whole volume, Mr. Root shows himself to be a bold and independent thinker, proceeding on original lines; and his work will well repay study by all who are interested in national economics, industry, and commerce."

*Bradford Observer.*—"We close this interesting and instructive volume with the thought of the ever-increasing complexity of commercial questions deeply stamped upon the mind. For this book is not the work of a professed student of economics, politics, or history, but of an educated, thoughtful, and observant man, engaged in an active business career. Yet he has found it impossible to discuss his subject adequately without an equipment in these sciences, which would give him honours in any examination upon them. The assumption that mere 'business capacity' is enough warrant to pronounce dogmatically on industrial and economic questions receives a crushing rebuke from such a volume as this."

*Scotsman.*—"There is much useful matter in the book, which is clearly the work of one who has thought out the questions, and who has gathered together a mass of useful statistics."

*Glasgow Herald.*—"Mr. Root is lucid, informing, and suggestive, and his book is well worth reading."

www.ingramcontent.com/pod-product-compliance
Lightning Source LLC
Chambersburg PA
CBHW031405160426
43196CB00007B/904